C
CHINESE
A
ARTS
&
L
LETTERS

中華人文

杨昊成 主编

Editor in Chief: Yang Haocheng

No. 1 2018

译林出版社

图书在版编目（CIP）数据

中华人文. 2018. 第1辑 / 杨昊成主编. —南京 ：译林出版社，2018.4

ISBN 978-7-5447-7341-6

Ⅰ.①中… Ⅱ.①杨… Ⅲ.①中华文化 Ⅳ.①K203

中国版本图书馆 CIP 数据核字（2018）第 080797 号

中华人文　杨昊成 / 主编

责任编辑　於　梅
装帧设计　韦　枫
责任印制　董　虎

出版发行　译林出版社
地　　址　南京市湖南路 1 号 A 楼
邮　　箱　yilin@yilin.com
网　　址　www.yilin.com
市场热线　025-86633278
排　　版　南京展望文化发展有限公司
印　　刷　江苏凤凰扬州鑫华印刷有限公司
开　　本　718 毫米 ×1000 毫米 1/16
印　　张　13.25
版　　次　2018 年 4 月第 1 版　2018 年 4 月第 1 次印刷
书　　号　ISBN 978-7-5447-7341-6
定　　价　88.00 元

Editorial Office of CHINESE ARTS & LETTERS

Editor in Chief : Yang Haocheng
Deputy Editors in Chief (alphabetically) : Jia Mengwei Josh Stenberg Liu Feng
Editors : Han Lifeng Xu Shiyan
Director of Editorial Office : Li Zhongtao
Edited by School of Foreign Languages & Cultures, Nanjing Normal University
Address: 1 Wenyuan Road, Huacheng Hall, Nanjing Normal University, Nanjing, P.R. China (210023)
Phone: 86-25-85891029
E-mail: chineseartsletters@njnu.edu.cn; chineseartsletters@163.com
Website: http://english.jschina.com.cn/chineseartsletters
Published by Yilin Press.
Address: Buiding A, 1 Hunan Road, Nanjing, P. R. China (210009)
Phone: 86-25-86633278
Cover Calligraphy: Yang Haocheng
Cover Design: Wei Feng

《中华人文》编辑部

主编：杨昊成
副主编（按拼音排序）：贾梦玮 刘 锋 石峻山
编辑：韩丽枫 许诗焱
编辑部主任：李钟涛
编辑单位：南京师范大学外国语学院
出版单位：译林出版社
封面题字：杨昊成
封面设计：韦 枫
地址：中国南京市湖南路1号A楼（210009）
电话：86-25-85891029
邮箱：chineseartsletters@njnu.edu.cn; chineseartsletters@163.com
网址：http://english.jschina.com.cn/chineseartsletters

Contents

Apr. 30
2018
VOL 5
NO. 1
TOTAL 9

Editor's Note

Editor in Chief
Yang Haocheng / 杨昊成

To be frank, I started reading Ye Mi (叶弥) only a little over three years ago when she was recommended to me by both Su Tong (苏 童) and Fan Xiaoqing (范小青), who said that she was a writer of real narrative power with a unique style of her own. The first story I read of hers and then published in *CAL* is "Family," one that is vastly different from others in that it smacks of a strong flavor of the ambiance prevalent in the writings of the Republican period of China. Her mind seems to me to be totally engrossed in a serene world far away from the madding crowd of today. Mountains and flowers, temples and monasteries, the bright moon and a sprinkling of lonely, leisurely souls—all these seem to have made up the entire world of her literary landscape. She is instinctively attached to these things and people and seems to have little interest in what is going on in this world of mundane existence. I've always been wondering what could possibly be the reason behind this literary preference of hers. Then I was reminded of her retreat from the city to the countryside a few years ago, where she preferred a self-contained, rustic life with her patches of vegetables and fruit trees and flocks of fowls and pets. Ye Mi is my age and not that old to retire to the country like China's reputed recluses of the olden days when they had either suffered enough setbacks in the realistic world, or when they were tired of the schemes and struggles of the outside world and dreamed of withdrawing to the mountains and waters for an unperturbed life. Ye Mi seems to fit into neither category. But then who knows! What I do know is that the female author is very happy with what she has and what she is. She is at present the proud master of her own house at the side of the Taihu Lake, now working in the fields, now walking with her cherished pets, but most of the time peacefully working away at her letters.

Starting this issue, *CAL* has a new column added to it: "Echoes of Classics." We'll pick and choose those cultural and literary gems throughout the history of Chinese civilization from Laozi's *Daodejing*, Confucius' *Analects*, the pre-Qin prose, the works of the Pléiade of the Bamboo Grove, Tang and Song poetry, Yuan drama, Ming and Qing fiction, all the way down to the May 4th literary masterpieces. For *Daodejing*, which is the first on our long list and is known to have been the most translated Chinese classic with one hundred versions or so in English alone, we hesitated a lot as to which of these renditions to choose. James Legge? Frederic Henry Balfour? Witter Bynner? Arthur Waley? Lin Yutang (林语堂)? Or D.C. Lau (刘殿爵)? All towering figures in sinology or literary translation, but finally we came down to Bill Porter, a.k.a. Red Pine, a name with some Zen implication in it which Porter adopted for himself after more than a dozen years of life and work in Taiwan and Hong Kong. His rendition of *Daodejing*, using simple enough English to capture the austere and sometimes elusive meaning of the original text, impresses me as having the advantage of better fluidity in reading and easier accessibility to the modern reader. What is more noteworthy is his eclectic selection from the ocean of literary commentaries and exegeses on *Daodejing* throughout Chinese literary history which is yet another sure evidence of Porter's extensive reading and rigorous scholarship. *Dadejing*, like *The Analects*, with its colloquial style, is relatively a simple text, but translating it is by no means easy. That's why the Canadian sinologist W.A.C.H. Dobson, whose translation of *Mencius* won him world-wide accolade, said that it was time for a sinologist to retire when he announced that he was working on a new version of *Daodejing*. We don't know exactly what is behind Dobson's words, but we are moved by Porter's courage to take up the challenge of translating this *Daoist* classic at an age when most people would prefer a cozy, retired life with their family and yet he decided to follow the dictates of his heart and set his mind on burning the long, solitary midnight oil.

One of the problems prior to translating *Daodejing* is that the translator will come across different versions of the text, including different punctuations, for throughout the ages, the text of *Daodijing* underwent numerous recensions and each would claim itself to be authentic. This alone will result in different enough interpretations and accordingly, divergent renditions. I take this to be quite normal with most ancient texts. Porter claims to have compared several dozen versions of the original and we respect his final choice of the version to base his translation on.

The whole text of *Daodejing*, which is made up of the Scriptures of *Dao* (Way) and the Scriptures of *De* (Virture), has 81 chapters in all and approximately 5,400 words. It is impossible to have the entire text and its English equivalent printed here in *CAL*. Besides, some sayings are more or less redundant semantically. We've picked those most well-known sayings, 16 chapters in all, for our readers. For those who care to do further comparative research on the classic, we've put the original Chinese alongside its English translation. And to make the Chinese look more like a *bona fide* original text, we've arranged it in the traditional rather than the simplified script and on a vertical setting of types. This arrangement will remain unchanged with all the other Chinese texts in "Echoes of Classics" that are to follow. Porter's illuminating Introduction to Laozi, *Daodejing* and his translation of the work in Mercury House in 1996 is also printed here for those who might be first readers of this *Daoist* classic.

And a bit of change to one of *CAL*'s regular columns "Articles." Renamed "Culture and Heritage," this column, self-evidently more revealing by the sheer name of it, will include anything written, or translated, about Chinese culture at large, regardless of genre, style, time period, or subject matter. "The Essentials of Chinese Calligraphy," my piece based on my two Dartmouth lectures during my one-year stint as a post-doc at Harvard twelve years ago, is printed here for the scrutinizing eye of both the professionals and common lovers of Chinese calligraphy. Comprised of three parts, viz., Evolution, Aesthetic, and Technique, the article is meant not as a pure academic research into one of the most abstract forms of traditional Chinese art, but as a primary on a brief history of calligraphy, on how calligraphy is usually appreciated, and how calligraphy is normally practiced. Each and every word is spoken from my thirty-odd years of experience of daily practice and I hope I'm not blowing my own trumpet.

The short story in this issue is Pang Yu's (庞羽) "Wealth, Blessings and Longevity." As a young writer of the post-90s generation, Pang is a rising star in contemporary Chinese literary arena, and her style is easily recognizable for its raciness and saltatory way of thinking and word manipulation. Not easy to translate though, and that's why we've asked Denis Mair, one of our most adept and exact translators, to do the job, and even he acknowledged to have to "wrestle with the picturesqueness of the language" in order to best preserve its "folksy charm."

One needs a pair of poetic eyes to see the extraordinary

through the ordinary, and that's the case with Hu Xian (胡弦), the featured poet of this issue of *CAL*. There really is nothing remarkably stunning about the things he writes about, pebbles, trees, clouds, roads, spiders, circus troupes, fish on a chopping board, etc., but our poet has unusually keen antennae for the nature of these insignificant things or their facets easily ignored by us commoners. Even the decadent is transformed into the magical, as "Insects in Amber" well manifests, and that's what poetry is all about, I guess.

After a whole three years of reticence, Shen Li (沈黎) resurfaces with her short piece on Lin Fengmian (林风眠), one of the most successful Sinicizers of western painting tradition of 20th century China. Lin was a very lonely man throughout most of his career; he was active in the artistic circles only in his early and later life, but other than that, he was rejected and marginalized, even maltreated in his prime years largely due to the ignorance of his contemporaries. Paradoxically, however, the misfortune turned out to be an actual blessing. Pushed to the limbo, away from all the hustle and bustle in the mainstream, Lin was able to settle down to the ontological study and practice of painting. And faced with seemingly endless days and months to kill, he produced one after another the most dazzling works of art ranging from fishing villages, birds and trees, old-day maids to Peking opera figures, female nudes and still life of all kinds. Not until his octogenarian years though did he enjoy a triumphant comeback and a universal recognition as one of the few genuine masters of 20th century Chinese art history.

Lin's works are particular about conveying verve and technique, stressing a lot the unity of truthfulness and ornamentation. With his dense composition and oftentimes heavy ink and bright colors, his works would shine with tenderness out of strong contrast, richness out of simplicity. Shen Li's article "Coffee Pot or Water Jug?" on Lin's still life, catches but a tip of the iceberg, a drop in the ocean of the artist's prodigious repertoire, but the glassware with its "glistening transparency" to which the artist is drawn seems to be equally intriguing to the author. With her expert eye for art and her brilliant writing to express her views on art, Shen shows us the possibility of a fine example of art criticism. And, indeed, an English scholar with an acute artistic sensibility like her is definitely hard to come by.

Featured Author: Ye Mi
（叶　弥）

Ye Mi, whose original name was Zhou Jie, was born in Suzhou in 1964. She started writing novels in 1994. A member of the Plenary Committee of Chinese Writers' Association, she also serves as Vice Chairperson of Jiangsu Writers' Association. Her works, which won her various prizes, including the Sixth Lu Xun Literature Prize, have been introduced into other nations such as UK, USA, France, Japan, Russia, Germany and South Korea. Now Ye Mi lives by the Taihu Lake in Suzhou.

Ye Mi / 叶弥

Bright Moon Temple

Ye Mi / 叶　弥
Translated by Ella Schwalb

In springtime, when the sunshine was goading all kinds of flowers to struggle into bloom, I slung my backpack over my shoulder and left home. I wanted to go see the blossoms. The season was sure to lose its pristine sparkle in two weeks' time—many flowers would start to wilt on their branches, and petals would fall to the dust in droves. So I wanted to take it all in before the spring turned dull and dirty, to see how the flowers blossomed. Once this moment passed, would there be anything left blooming for me to see?

My aim was simple. I squinted in the sun as it shone down on my face, and then I leisurely set out, heading south.

I got to some mountains after a while. Peach blossoms stretched as far as the eye could see, and the earth and sky were all flooded with sun as the sweet wind drifted by above the flowering trees. In the soft, warm chuckle of that all-pervasive sunshine, I ceased to exist, my steps light and buoyant as though I were the sun's own two feet.

I was walking along when someone behind me said, "Hey there, where are you headed?"

I turned around and saw a swarthy old villager with a stick-straight back walking behind me.

"I'm taking a springtime

walk," I said.

I hung back a bit, and the old man caught up to me.

"You've come from the city," he concluded confidently. Then he continued, as though talking to himself, "I'm just coming back from the city myself. I went yesterday on a transport ship that belongs to a relative, so I got a free ride. I started back first thing this morning, and caught a little town bus, but they wanted to charge me twelve yuan. I got mad, and got off halfway without paying them even one cent. That's how I managed to save twelve yuan on my way there, and then six more on my way back."

I laughed to myself. He peered at my face, then said earnestly, "Nobody comes by these parts, as there are no touristic sites here. It has been an obscure locale from time immemorial." I couldn't help but let out a great belly laugh when I heard the old man putting on airs like this. But he didn't pay me any mind, and just went on talking, "Erlang Mountain is the only good thing to see. Bright Moon Temple is up there, and there are lots of flowering plants and bamboo. There are pheasants too, and to the south and east of the mountain there's a lake with wild ducks in it. People say that if the pheasants mate with the ducks, they make a phoenix... yes, this mountain is well worth seeing, so you might as well go up and take a look around. You can stay in the temple for twenty yuan a night, three meals included. The only people up there are the couple who run the temple. They used to be regular folk—from the city, like you. They came in the spring of 1970, but nobody knows why. It's been almost thirty years now, and they've never had any family come to visit... The man is named Master Luo, and the woman Master Bo, and even though they run the temple, they still dress like commoners and live together as husband and wife, sleeping in the same room and everything. Isn't that strange?"

As he spoke, the old villager hurried forward a little until he was a few paces ahead of me. Holding both hands behind his back, he said, "Come with me.

Master Luo came down the mountain today, he's doing a ritual to send off a ghost from Tugen's house. You can eat lunch there, and then follow Master Luo when he goes back up the mountain."

I couldn't help but ask, "And where do you live, neighbor?"

"Not far," he said, "Bright Moon Village, right under Erlang Mountain."

Seeing that he had taken it upon himself to be my host, I followed this old stranger without saying a word.

We quickly reached the village, which was small and walled-in by mountains on three sides. Children, chickens, ducks, and dogs were all roaming about every which way. It was almost lunchtime, and the scene was rife with that pre-meal bustle. In the open space in front of a family home, I saw an old man with a red shirt and green pants sitting solemnly upright on a bench. There were a few other benches set up in front of him, all filled with the village's menfolk, old and young alike. All I could make out was the old man's loud voice:

"Humans must not get arrogant. When a human is arrogant, he ceases to resemble a human, and does harm unto others. Ghosts must never get arrogant either, or else they will do harm too, just like humans."

The listeners all nodded their heads together in assent. Then, the old man in the red shirt and green pants pressed both hands down on his lap, and crooned in a half-song:

Three types of meat and three vegetables

Oh, a duck, and rice in a bowl

Of wooden chopsticks take a bunch

And place them neatly on your lunch...

Eighteen dumplings shaped like rings

Thirteen dumplings wrapped in leaves...

And now the ghost of life and death

Takes his leave, and heads northwest...

Each line that the old fellow in the red shirt and green pants intoned was met with the "Got it" of a stocky middle-aged man.

"That's Mr. Luo there, in the red shirt and green pants," explained the old man who had led me. "And the man responding to him is Tugen ... Hey, Tugen, I've brought someone from the city. She'll eat at your house, and then she'll go up with Master Luo to spend the night on the mountain."

And that's how I met Master Luo and Master Bo. As I mentioned, my reason for traveling was very simple, so it didn't matter to me where I wound up. All I wanted was to see some flowers, and it didn't make any difference whom I followed. And besides, I liked the idea of going to a temple so I could consult some divination sticks, to ask a little something about love.

Master Luo couldn't have been more different from that other old man—he was taciturn and melancholy every step of the way. I heard him hum a couple lines of a song but I couldn't hear it clearly, and seeing as he didn't like to talk, I didn't think it appropriate to ask him what it was. My first take on him was that he was a depressed old man who had suffered injustice; his life story was a bit of a mystery, yet everything about his current situation smacked of an ordinary, mundane existence. His red coat and green pants looked strange and naive against the pink peach blossoms that covered the mountain. I walked behind him, watching his nimble gait and the constant sway of his loose red coat and green trousers, like two points of colored light, coupled together as they leapt along the mountain path. Maybe he is a jolly, simple person after all, without much of a past to speak of, I thought. He's been here thirty years in a state of fundamental waiting. Or maybe he even refused some sort of glory...

We reached the bamboo forest at the top of the mountain, and Bright Moon Temple came in and out of view between the stalks. It was a small temple, and its old, yellowed paint bore the marks of many years of daily toil and soot from cooking fires and burning incense. When I went inside, everything was dark and it took a moment before my eyes adjusted enough to see the furnishings. A towering wooden shrine in the middle of the room displayed the Goddess of Mercy, the Savior of the Suffering, behind which I saw a hallway that probably led to the guest room. On nights when the moon is out, I mused, that whole lonesome hallway must be soaked through with moonlight.

I was anxious to meet Master Bo.

She came out from behind the wooden shrine—I knew it was her the moment I saw her. She was a lean old lady with a slight, meager frame and slight, meager hair. Her skin was grayish, ashy-pale, a perfect match for this gloomy room. She had a singularly clear and bright expression in her eyes, and her look was one of unswerving concentration. Those eyes seemed to contain a great deal of importance—but a closer look revealed that there was nothing more than that stream of tenderness that flowed out from her gaze like water, seeping out in a warmth that slowly and imperceptibly permeated everything. It was a pure and refreshing osmosis, an irresistible infiltration.

The moonlight that fell upon Bright Moon Temple was probably quite similar.

"Do you want to draw a divination stick?" she asked, looking at me. "My divination sticks here in this temple are different from those you'll find elsewhere," she added. "They aren't split up into top, middle, and bottom. So long as there's something in there that's even a little useful to you, that's your top stick."

So I burned incense and touched my head to the floor in front of the Goddess of Mercy. Then I pulled out a divination stick from the bamboo tube. It read:

A looming mirage
Mist past eyes
Fallen flowers, flowing water
Life floats like a dream

An insuppressible mournfulness suddenly came over me: we humans destroy everything we create. But we cannot simply stop creating, because then what would there be to destroy?

Master Bo gave me another thoughtful look and said, "Drawing divination sticks is like reading a book: it's best somewhere between belief and disbelief."

"So when it comes down to it," I asked, "is that believing or not?"

"I can't explain," she said, the hint of a smile crossing her pale white face. Then she added, "I was just like you when I was your age, always wanting to draw sharp lines between things."

I got the sudden sense that Master Bo might have been a teacher in the past. And if she had in fact been a teacher, she would certainly have taught literature and languages. I immediately shared my insight with Master Bo. She looked alarmed at first, and then happy. But that joyful look only just barely brushed across her face before quickly being replaced by a faint dolefulness.

I figured I had unintentionally stirred up some sorrow that she kept stored away deep in her heart. I didn't mean to. In all the years she'd been in this temple, perhaps nobody had ever touched that old wound. And if that were the case, then in fact it must have been fate that brought me to her, because I caught sight of her sorrow ever so slightly. I had discovered it by accident, and felt pangs of regret.

She didn't say yes and she didn't say no. She didn't say anything at all.

But when I found myself at a loss for what to say, Master Bo offered, "Come with me, I'll show you the flowers I grow."

She led me around the wooden shrine to the hallway. The hall was wide and winding, and so old that all the paint had peeled off from the pillars and the eaves. The floor was laid with gray bricks, many of which were broken, and there was moss growing between their cracks, crawling along the seams and up the whitewashed walls. She kept pointing things out to me along the way: this is the guest room, here's the bedroom she shares with Master Luo, this is the kitchen, that's the dining room. There were some other small rooms, whose designated purposes remained obscure, where lumber and ropes were piled haphazardly, or vegetables laid out to dry. All in all, it looked like a typical living environment. Master Bo and Master Luo were just a regular old country couple.

When we got to the eastern end of the hall, Master Bo opened a door onto a passageway—a slightly sloping sunny hillside sat right outside the back door, and below Bright Moon Lake stretched as far as the eye could see. Naturally, my eye went first to the lake, and from there I was drawn to the fields on the hillside. Every little plot of vegetables and flowers was so meticulously tended that it looked like they'd been smoothed over by hand, day after day. Seeing all this, I got the sense again that Master Luo and Master Bo were no different than those ordinary couples that lived down the mountain, enjoying all kinds of simple and bright earthly pleasures, and I quit making conjectures about what kinds of secrets their past held. Making conjectures is a gloomy business.

I have always loved flowers, and to see them in blossom was the very reason I had gone on this trip in the first place. The flowers on the sunny slope were blooming in a brilliant display of colors. There were many that I didn't recognize, which was no surprise given that Master Bo told me she had transplanted most of them from farther up in the mountains, including one species called JianChunLuo.

She specially pointed it out to me.

I carefully examined this yellow flower called JianChunLuo. With its shockingly slender stalk, it resembled a Qing Dynasty woman wearing a very high scalloped collar. Its crown, too, resembled a Qing woman's subtle expressiveness: just a scant few petals on its bright yellow face, with the unmistakable look of wanting to say something, but holding back.

I told Master Bo that I liked the "pungent" flora that was wantonly blooming over there. I liked how carefree they looked.

Master Bo went off to

the field to pick a few little cabbages. I could tell she was a bit put off, and realized I must have said something she didn't like. I was quick to offer up a joke. "Oh, I know. 'JianChunLuo' has 'Luo' in it. 'Luo' like Master Luo—you must plant this flower especially for him."

Squatting in the field, she laughed without looking at me, her face turned instead towards the vegetables on the ground. Her laughter was thoroughly heartfelt and her face even got a bit red. I could tell by her smile that it was rare for her to laugh so heartily—the corners of her mouth were rigid, and the wrinkles around her eyes and mouth were all uncooperative. It may well have been heartfelt, but it didn't look very natural.

This joke had earned her approval.

She started to relax entirely. She walked quickly in front of me, vegetable basket in hand, and from behind, I could see in her agility a lithe gracefulness very rare for someone her age. Seeing such gracefulness was enough for me to conclude that she had been a great beauty in her youth, doted on by all.

A beauty past her prime, spending her remaining years tranquil in a temple. Was it fortune? Or was it misfortune?

Master Bo walked past Master Luo, who was sweeping the courtyard floor. Without looking at him, she thought aloud, "Our girl here said that I planted JianChunLuo especially for you."

Master Luo replied as though he were coughing to himself, "I think so too."

The connection between them was such that they could communicate without even looking at each other.

I wasn't used to this mode of talking, and was worried they would use it with me, too.

Master Bo cooked up some rice and vegetables, Master Luo finished tidying up the courtyard, and I got settled into the guest room. We were like a family of three as we all gathered around to eat at the small kitchen table. I've never liked the dining room for eating in earnest.

"Darling," Master Bo called to me, looking at me with that fluid glance of hers—precisely the kind of communication I preferred. She called me so softly that my heart ached, as though I had heard my own mother calling to me from afar. My hands trembled as they cupped the rice bowl. It dropped to the table with a "clack."

"Eat up," she said.

"Stop telling her to eat," said Master Luo. "Tell her to look at the clouds outside the window."

Outside the west-facing kitchen window, the mountain was full of beautiful flowers in many hues and the sky above showed still more magnificent colors. It was no more than a day coming to its end, but the sky made it look like there would be no tomorrow, giving its all for this dazzling curtain call. So we watched the beautiful rosy sunset—so sweet it was wistful.

The lantern gave off a dim yellow light. I was astonished by how quickly day turned to night here on the mountain. The sky got dark in no time, and after that the dim yellow lighting seemed bright.

"How romantic, Master Luo," I said. "No wonder Master Bo planted those JianChunLuo for you."

They both looked at me, smiling.

Both of them wanted to speak, and of course so did I. We looked just like a family of three, reunited and with so much to say to each other.

"Dear Master Luo here likes to watch me whenever I wash my feet," said Master Bo. "He loves my feet."

"You have good-looking feet," said Master Luo. "Why don't you take off your shoes and let her see?"

"This won't do," she said.

"What's the big deal about looking at feet?"

"No, this won't do at all."

I was a little baffled at how a husband and wife could talk so intimately in my presence, completely uninhibited. But I was relieved when I saw in their expressions that they didn't seem to be flirting. In my relief I thought how sincere they both were. I wasn't used to this kind of sincerity, estranged from it as

I was by my own desires.

Changing the subject, I asked Master Luo, "Down the mountain, are all the ceremonies for driving off ghosts alike? Do you believe in ghosts?"

Master Luo replied, "There are lots of different tricks for driving off ghosts. I just do my version. And I can't quite say whether or not ghosts exist. As I see it, we'd better not have ghosts. People in this world already live in such a hideous mess, so wouldn't adding ghosts into the mix just make things even more difficult?... Humans really can't get arrogant..."

Master Bo jumped in, "In my opinion it's better if we do have ghosts, because that would mean we could be reunited with many people who have died. When people die they turn into ghosts, and when ghosts die they turn into *jian*. It's an endless cycle of reincarnation, to redeem the wrongs you've done."

Master Bo's words stirred up a question in me. I asked cautiously, "What kinds of things count as wrongs?"

At this point, we had already finished eating. It all seemed familiar somehow—the smells wafting out from the rice and vegetable bowls set aside on the table, the bare-bones lighting above our heads, the still-warm cooking fire in the hearth, and the old-fashioned table and drab walls. Everything about it created a calming ambience.

It was the ideal setting to pose the question I had just asked.

The line came back to me: "What kinds of things count as wrongs?"

The question had sunk the room into a sudden spell of silence. The silence arose abruptly, but it made sense, I thought. We all felt that we'd been brought together by fate, and there was too much we wanted to say to each other. We fell into a strange position: in that brief moment that had just flitted by, we all longed for one another.

But we just stared at each other, and nobody said a word. Bygone dreams swept by like precious fleeting glances.

Master Luo stood up first. He sighed and left, followed by Master Bo who went to the hearth to clean up. Like a thief, I slipped away to the hallway and returned to my room.

I spread the blanket out on the bed, then washed my hair and bathed. It was pitch black outside, and the mountain was silent. I took out my notebook to record the day's events, but as soon as I got to writing down what I remembered, the mountain was peaceful no more: a big, yellow full moon had come out from the east, and lay suspended in the low tree branches. It must have risen up out of the lake, I thought. It's too bad I missed seeing the way it broke the water's surface. Moonlight is actually a most disturbing substance. That's why Ming scholar Zhang Dai said that people from Hangzhou avoid the moon like they avoid their enemies.

I left the room and walked through the hall to the passageway that we had taken to the sunny hillside. The door was already closed, and as I reached out to undo the bolt, my hand came across something on the wall that left my fingers tingling. My instinct was one of abhorrence and fear—I rashly let out a loud "Augh!"

Hearing my cry, Master Luo and Master Bo came out. They were still dressed neatly in all their clothes, which meant they hadn't yet gone to bed.

Master Luo switched on a flashlight and shined it at the wall, revealing a crawling mass of tiny praying mantises about the size of soybeans, all packed densely together. It was a little mantis nest. "Merciful Buddha!" Master Bo exclaimed.

I stealthily flicked a dead mantis off my finger to the ground.

Master Luo turned off the flashlight, and the three of us stood there exchanging glances, speechless once more. Then, Master Bo asked, "Is it the eighteenth day of the lunar month?"

"It's the seventeenth," answered Master Luo.

"Let's take our girl to the lakeside to go look at the moon," said Master Bo.

Once outside, Master Bo turned abruptly towards Master Luo and said, "Why don't you go back and fetch your bamboo flute so you can play? We'll wait for you on the dock."

The night wind soughed and sighed as we walked across a short stretch of stone steps that led to the lakeside. The so-called dock was nothing more than a little mud dike that stretched out towards the middle of the lake. Perhaps it had been a dock for mooring fishing boats in some distant time, but now it was completely useless, remarkably peaceful there in the moonlight. On careful reflection, its past and present must have been a close echo of the life trajectory of my two hosts.

We stood by the lakeside for a while. The moon moved from the low thicket on the east and rose till it reached the tall treetops. There was another moon steeped in water within the lake, strange in shape and texture. A gust of wind blew past, and a din sounded through the bamboo forest as though hordes of cavalry were galloping past with frightening momentum. When the wind calmed, the trees stopped moving, and the sound of Master Luo's bamboo flute could be heard.

It was much more resonant than I had imagined—he played straight into the night air. Anyone who plays a tone with such loud intensity must have harbored some ambitions in his past, and must be haunted now by bitterness. But for what?

What with the lake water, the bright moon, and the sound of the flute, for a moment I didn't know where I was.

I wanted to understand them, and resolved to venture another question.

We went back on that same stone path. Master Luo waited for us, and Master Bo took her hand away from mine and gave it to him. Hand in hand, they walked ahead of me in silence, and I knew they were alone in this moonlight; I had ceased to exist.

Back in the hallway, there was no moonlight and I couldn't see their faces as they stood in the doorway. There was one room that separated their room from my own. Tomorrow I would be leaving, and now it was time to sleep. If I didn't ask now, I would never have another chance. I'd be satisfied with a single sentence, or half a sentence—even the slightest disclosure of the faintest hint.

I turned to them and said, "Master Bo, people say you two came here in the spring of 1970. It's been thirty years, and no one has ever come to visit you."

Master Bo immediately looked to Master Luo, who quickly pulled her into their room, and bolted up the door in a flurry. All this happened in the space of one distracted blink, and by the time I realized what was happening, the door was already closed. I stood in the hallway completely dull, feeling a twinge of guilt.

I had been sleeping fitfully for who knows how long, when I was awakened by a sound. I opened my eyes and saw the sleek moonlight outside, shining as bright as day. The wind had stopped, and all the trees and clusters of flowers stood upright and still. Full of dread, I perked up my ears and listened closely to find out where the sound was coming from. I heard a weeping sound, as delicate as silk ... That's right, it was the sound of weeping, coming from Master Bo and Master Luo's room.

I walked toward their room and peered through the curtains, which hadn't been pulled closed. All I could see was Master Bo and Master Luo holding each other tight and crying. They were huddled so close, like they were cold.

Master Luo saw me off down the mountain early the next morning. The warm, pure, golden sunshine beamed down on the dew-covered mountain, and the droplets glistened and shone. The trees and flowers were at their peak clean freshness—a gift from heaven for humankind. I admired it as I walked, and though I got far I could still see Master Bo's figure standing in the temple doorway, her eyes wide open as she looked down at us from on high.

Master Luo escorted me to the foothills. He asked solemnly, "When will you be back?"

"One month, or maybe two," I answered noncommittally.

"Master Bo and I will be waiting for you," he said. As he spoke, the frailty of his many years showed on his face—resigned, at peace. When I saw him there—warm, neat, and forlorn—I understood perfectly well the yearning he was feeling as we parted ways.

I headed back on the same path I had taken to come, and resumed the same effortlessness of the day before. I flung my brief sojourn on Erlang Mountain to the back of my mind. With my backpack on, squinting against the sun, I moved as though I were sleepwalking—a world of difference from the vast uneasiness I had felt while on the mountain. Flowers may come each and every year, but they are never the same from one year to the next. At last I was enjoying the present.

I ran into that swarthy old villager again along the way. "Going back, huh?" he asked me cheerfully.

"Yes, going back," I said.

"Did you see any phoenixes up on the mountain?" he asked.

"No, I didn't," I said.

"Alas, the pheasants of the mountain and the wild ducks of the lake were not willing to mate," he said with regret. Then he told me, "I'm heading to Far Misty Village at the foot of Far Misty Mountain. An old friend of mine has been quarreling with his daughter-in-law and he's so worked up that he won't even eat. I'm going to try and help him smooth things over. If you're free, you should come along for the fun."

"Did the ghost leave Tugen's house after all?" I asked.

"Yes, yes, he left yesterday afternoon," he replied. Then he turned off down a fork in the road and was gone.

I was in an extraordinarily pleasant mood, so once I got home it never occurred to me to go back to Erlang Mountain.

Elusive Erlang Mountain.

One, then two months passed in a flash. Spring and summer came and went so fast they didn't leave so much as a trace. It wasn't until autumn had arrived in full force, everything ablaze before coming to its end, that I suddenly remembered my promise.

I put on my backpack and sauntered leisurely the whole way, just like I had the previous spring. Last time had been a chance encounter, while this time I was making a special visit. Last time had been green; this time was golden. I didn't run into that swarthy old villager.

I made my own way up Erlang Mountain.

From the path I made out Bright Moon Temple. It was surrounded by scaffolding with lots of workers bustling around underneath. As I drew near the temple, a foreman-looking type came up to me and said, "I'm sorry, the temple is being renovated. Construction personnel only. It's going to be a proper Buddhist temple—the higher-ups will appoint lots of monks to beat out a chanting rhythm, and they'll also choose an official Head Monk."

This didn't sound good. "What about Master Luo and Master Bo?" I asked, "I know them well."

"Know them well, eh?" the foreman said. "Knowing them well won't do anybody any good. Master Bo died two months ago, and Master Luo left a month later. Master Bo was deathly ill—she kept getting thinner and thinner until she looked like a brittle winter leaf that had fallen to the ground. Master Luo has gone to Fragrant Flower Temple on Gulang Island to formally become a monk. His religious name is Hui Chen, Intelligent Dust."

Intelligent Dust? Of course.

And that was that. A slice of my past.

As for the past within the past—I cannot say. Who were Master Luo and Master Bo after all? What kinds of secrets did they have? And what had they lived through? Nobody knows, and I can only get the faintest sense of it: it seems like it had something to do with forgiveness, with redemption, with waiting... and naturally it was about love and hate as well. What a pity I didn't go back to Erlang Mountain in time. I'm convinced that if I'd gone up again, they would have told me all the secrets in Bright Moon Temple—oh, they had so much more to say!

Bright Moon Temple cannot speak.

Epilogue: That whole fall I was in low spirits, having a real bout of autumn blues. I made a few fruitless efforts to make sense of the riddles of Master Luo and Master Bo's past. I went to the district records office to look up local news from the spring of 1970. As you know, government archives of district records are pretty unwieldy, by and large. This one was a chart that wasn't organized by year, but rather divided up horizontally according to so-called subject matter, such as "Agriculture Chronicle," "Industry Chronicle," "Population Chronicle," and so on, with the accounts written vertically below. This all left me wholly unsatisfied. Once, in some out-of-the-way town, I saw a local chronicle from the Republic of China era that had been compiled by a few scholars back then. The content included what time the rooster crowed at some house in some village; what day of what year some lonely village widow finally got remarried; the year that the first spring thunderstorm struck three people dead... It was all extremely fascinating. Local chronicles don't collect stuff like that nowadays.

I didn't turn up anything useful.

But once, I was invited to a relative's dinner party. At the banquet, there was an old gentleman in his eighties, with sharp ears and keen eyes. I asked him if he still remembered any interesting things that had happened in the city during the spring of 1970.

"Oh, plenty," he said. Then he leaned in close to my ear, and cheerfully recounted all sorts of tales of the town: of murder, and of disobedience and betrayal, of heartbreak and elopement, and of house fires and thievery... As I listened, I kept thinking to myself that none of it had anything to do with those Masters, Luo and Bo... and that maybe it had everything to do with them.

2003

Snowflake Meditation

Ye Mi / 叶　弥
Translated by Ella Schwalb

Man wants to make a battlefield of everything, and the realm of social relations is no exception. But when the real war came, He Wenjian wanted to run off to Xi'an.

Despite the chaos, many people in Wuguo came out to show their respect as news of his planned departure spread, braving the dangers of Japanese bombardment to pay him a farewell visit. Yesterday, in the middle of all the hubbub, somebody had hung up a banner outside his study. It read:

"Without you, the city will be empty."

He Wenjian cried when he saw the banner, knowing the vengefulness of those words. Wuguo sat at the edge of Shanghai, which had fallen into enemy hands the day before. It was only a matter of time before Wuguo followed suit, and now he intended to flee.

The past few days had been an endless stream of bitter farewells and He Wenjian was worn out both mentally and physically. He Wenjian didn't like death, and he didn't like saying goodbye. What he liked was being on his own turf, free and easy, enjoying the finer things in life. After all, there was quite a lot to enjoy: in the He family stable, there was a pair of enormous horses who let out mighty snorts from time to time, and the first motorcar in all of Wuguo was parked next to the fountain in the courtyard, with a chauffeur hired from Shanghai. There were two bicycles that often leaned, glistening, against the rockery, and a rickshaw that was always parked by the gate. Little Jiang, who pulled the rickshaw, also worked as the family's gardener. In the backyard there was a palanquin that could be carried by four people—the very one that He Wenjian's father used to use. Sometimes, instead of riding his horses, He Wenjian would go on outings sitting atop the palanquin, with a few servant girls walking alongside dressed in rich attire—some days all in *qipaos*, other days in Western fashions. In all of Wuguo, there was no one else who liked to enjoy himself this way. His painting boat was moored to the private dock behind the He residence, and he employed two chefs on board: one for light refreshments, and another for hot meals. On nights when the full moon shone clear and bright, he would invite three or five close friends to go out in his boat. The chefs would make food, the servant girls would pour wine, and they would eat their mung bean cakes as they quietly glided along the clear jade brook. The He family's backyard was lined with osmanthus flowers, magnolias, cape jasmines, honeysuckles and roses, and the fragrance of the flowers would roll gently by in the evening wind's soft caress, as they admired the moon in the sky and the lights along the river.

But the fun didn't stop there. Inside the house there were two big rooms: one where he kept everything he needed for his well-rounded repertoire of classic opera performances—his outfits, along with all sorts of musical instruments like zithers, drums, fiddles and *pipas*. He also liked to write and put on his own modern dramas. The other room held his beloved antiques, books, and calligraphy set—paper, inkstone, brush and ink—to equip him for writing, painting, and studying bronze inscriptions. Next to the fine rice paper, he kept his precious Leica with its Kodak lens. There wasn't another camera like it in all of Wuguo City. He used it to take photos of his wife and daughter, and of the servant girls.

The eve of his departure for Xi'an was a sentimental scene—the whole courtyard was abloom with wintersweet, and as he made his way through, it was as though he were wrapped up in a coat of dense fragrance.

Now, he was to bid farewell to this sweet, charmed life. He was fleeing. That last night, he wept himself to sleep.

He got up at the break of dawn, and burned Tibetan incense. Then he washed up, putting a few drops of his homemade rose water on his face towel. Next he drank half a small bowl of peach resin, royal jelly and osmanthus water that had been prepared for him in the kitchen. Breakfast was a poria porridge, dried shrimps tossed with parsley, and dried osmanthus-pickled eggplant, all of which he took with him to eat in the study.

His servant, Ah Jin, came into the room to announce that there were a few students who had come to the door, asking that Mr. He stand with Wuguo City to the bloody end.

He Wenjian listened, and after a long pause he said, "I can stand, sure. But to the bloody end? I still haven't thought it through enough to be certain. And even if I had thought it through, I'm afraid my body might not comply."

"What should I tell them?" asked Ah Jin.

"Go tell them that people have the right to exist, so long as they don't get in the way of other people's existence," said He Wenjian. "And people are free, so long as they don't break the law or betray their country. It's nobody's business what other people do."

Ah Jin said, "The wisdom of your words truly overwhelms me, Master. I fear I will forget them before I even reach the door."

When he got to the door, he said to the people outside, "Go on now, all of you. Our Master has said that rats leave a sinking ship, and everybody should get out while they still can."

Right as he finished

speaking, his forehead was struck by a rock. When he came back to his senses, the students were long gone and there was just a single figure standing before him, staring at him. It was Uncle Pan, whose nephew, Pan Xinbei, had been He Wenjian's best student. "What are you doing here, Uncle Pan?" asked Ah Jin.

"This may be foolish," said Uncle Pan. "But I know Mr. He is planning to leave, so I've come to ask for a few of the things he doesn't want."

"Have you no shame? There's no such thing in this whole house," said Ah Jin. "I've always said you were no good. If you'd been an upright person, you would have brought up Xinbei yourself, instead of abandoning him in Flower Temple when he was still so young. And now that His Lordship has picked up the slack and paid for him to go to school and make something of himself, you've got the nerve to drop in and try hobnobbing. You should be ashamed of yourself, really."

"It's not that I didn't raise him," said Uncle Pan, "I *couldn't* raise him. Blame it on his own bad luck for losing both parents when he was only six. Meanwhile, I still had four little ones of my own to provide for."

As he was talking, he fished out a big oval stone from his sleeve. "The political situation these days is such a mess that I always bring something like this along to defend myself any time I leave the house. Now you run along and tell the master I'm here, or else I'll treat you to another bump on the head."

Ah Jin went in and told He Wenjian, "Uncle Pan is here. He knows we're leaving and came to ask for a few of your belongings."

Hearing this, He Wenjian laughed. "He hasn't been by in a long time. Surely he's not just here to pick up some things. Bring him in."

When Uncle Pan entered the study, he saw He Wenjian eating what was left of the dried osmanthus-pickled eggplant. "I'm drooling," he said. "Won't you grant me a bite, Mr. He?" And without waiting for an answer, he grabbed the bowl and started eating.

He Wenjian didn't like these table manners. He turned away and looked instead at a hanging scroll painted by Tang Bohu. "What do you want?" he asked his guest.

"Favor me with a dining table, Sir. You can't possibly take them all with you," said Uncle Pan. "And every day, twice a day, my whole family gathers around the table together, young and old. It would be nice to have a good table."

He Wenjian's dining tables had all been carefully handpicked. As he mulled it over, Uncle Pan continued, "Or if Sir doesn't want to part with his tables, at least let me take that big catalpa tree that's out in the back garden. I'll just make my own table. No need to hem and haw or make excuses—in the havoc of wartime, all the trees in your garden will have to be chopped down to make gun handles sooner or later."

He Wenjian started to laugh. "I'm not making any excuses," he said. "Go ahead and take the catalpa tree. But tell me—everyone else is all worked up. How is it that you're so unfazed as to be in the market for a new table?"

Uncle Pan knelt down and touched his head to the floor. "Mr. He is truly an intelligent man. I will tell all," he said, without standing up. "Step outside, Ah Jin. You're just getting in the way by standing around here."

Ah Jin left. Then Uncle Pan got up and spoke, "As you know, Master He, my two buildings that face the street were bought by a Japanese man, Takeshita Shiro, to open Everlast Real Estate Company. He closed up shop early this spring and returned to Japan. But then, a few days ago, he came back again on the sly, bringing along a young Japanese guy. Shiro talked a lot, basically saying that people just need to take a realistic approach. He asked me to talk to you, to ask you not to go and to stay here to work with the Japanese in establishing the Joyful Land of Benevolent Greater East-Asian Reign."

"Ah, so you're a traitor," said He Wenjian. "So does that mean there are a lot of Japanese informers around now? Will the Japanese kill me if I leave Wuguo?"

"Shiro passed on a bit of information to me," said Uncle Pan. "He said that Yang Yinyu, the one who lives at Wuguo Bridge, studied abroad in Japan. But now she can't make heads or tails of Japan's Greater East-Asia plans, and she's been writing drivel in the papers nonstop. I'm afraid things won't end well for people like her. But you're an interesting, amiable guy, He, and you showed such kindness to my dear Xinbei. They won't dare touch you if you're with me. So if you want to go, just go quietly... I mean, if you decide not to go, then how am I supposed to make off with your catalpa tree?"

"Zhang Taiyan once told me something," said He Wenjian, "which is that small-town folk tend to think very highly of themselves."

"Thinking too highly of yourself is always better than not thinking highly enough," said Uncle Pan. "If you don't think highly of yourself, people just walk all over you."

"What perks are the Japanese giving you?" asked He Wenjian.

"It's too early to talk about perks," said Uncle Pan. "We'll just have to wait and see. The way I see it, it's only natural that man strives to move upward, just as water flows downward. They have power now and even the British, those old looters, can't do anything to stop them. The Americans are clearly scared too, what with their 'neutrality pact.' So we've got to rely on Japan. Mr. He, you're different from us common folk. If you cooperate with the Japanese, there's a whole lot to be gained."

He Wenjian lowered his head and sneered. Sipping his tea, he said, "The Japanese don't know anything besides war and killing. Gains or no gains, I couldn't possibly join them."

"In any case, I've told what I know," said Uncle Pan. "Ay, I'm backed into a corner myself—Shiro is pressing me hard, that cretin. Anyway, I'm off now to go get a gold tooth fitted. I've wanted one for a while... Well, have a nice trip!"

He Wenjian sat lost in thought. He was deeply distressed, unable to cry despite the urge. Then a sudden clamor sounded outside the door, and pointy-chinned Ah Jin ran in, deathly pale. He said, "Uncle Pan was stabbed to death on the street as soon as he left the gate... some people saw Pan Xinbei calling him to stop and chat, and then someone else scurried out from behind and stabbed him at least a dozen times—in the neck, the back, the waist... He didn't even get to take the catalpa tree. Oh merciful Buddha!"

"And what about Pan Xinbei?" asked He Wenjian.

"He ran off as soon as Uncle Pan hit the ground."

A voice came out from the bottom of the white marble steps that led to the study, "I'm right here, Mr. He."

It was Pan Xinbei.

Pan Xinbei had been Mr. He's best student. Both his parents died when he was six years old, so each month he would eat at the home of a different relative, while doing a few chores at Flower Temple in exchange for lodging there. When he was eight, he ran into He Wenjian, who was going to the temple to offer sacrifices to the flower spirits. He Wenjian saw that the boy was clever and quick-witted and decided to pay for his education. Pan Xinbei wasn't much to look at. He was slight and withered, and he always exuded a staggeringly bitter cold air, even when standing in the heat of the sun.

He Wenjian hadn't seen him in ages, and a trace of cowardice coursed through his whole being at the sight of him now. "Don't let him in," he said to Ah Jin. "His presence is too cold, and I have a bit of a headache. Have him go to the other room and give him some tea, and if he wants to talk, you can bring the messages back and forth."

The following dialogue was conveyed by Ah Jin, shuttling to and fro.

Pan Xinbei: "Please Ah Jin, tell our Master that he mustn't go. He must stay here and set a good example for the townspeople."

He Wenjian: "Ah Jin, go ask him if he's part of the anti-traitor brigade. I heard that there are anti-traitor brigades in both Shanghai and Beiping."

Pan Xinbei: "Yes, there are a few of us. Self-organized troops. The Japanese have already shed blood here in Wuguo, so it was time we got started ourselves."

He Wenjian: "Ah Jin, go ask him how he could bring himself to be an accomplice in the murder of his own uncle?"

Pan Xinbei: "The knife goes in clean and comes out red. Then you just wipe the blood off on your pant leg."

He Wenjian: "Wipe it off on your pant leg...? That's preposterous! Peasant behavior."

Ah Jin went to tell Pan Xinbei, "Wiping blood on your pants is unhygienic. Nobody should do such a thing—by city standards and rural standards alike."

"I can't stand this Pan fool," Ah Jin said to He Wenjian after a few more round trips. "He's got a real foul mouth on him, and now he's going on about all these noble patriots of the Song dynasty..."

"Don't pay him any mind. Let him curse if he wants," said He Wenjian, waving his hand. "Just go put more hot water in his teacup. His parents died young, leaving him all alone, and he's never had any hobbies or interests besides studying. This world has given him nothing to love. He has no fear of death. All he wants is to be a hero."

Ah Jin went back to the other room, and didn't return for a good long while.

"He pushed the teacup off to the floor and shattered it," he said, when he finally came back. "Then he bit into his gum and deliberately spat out a mouthful of blood onto the white wall..."

"All this blood and thunder, and the city hasn't even fallen into enemy hands yet," said He Wenjian.

"Oh, I forgot," said Ah Jin. "He also mentioned Master Wen Zhenheng who used to live at The Garden of Cultivation."

"I have nothing to learn from that romantic Wen Zhenheng, who went so far as to drown himself for the ideals of 'loyalty' and 'righteousness,' " said He Wenjian. "But everyone is free to do what they will—he was free to die, just as I am free to live."

The beaded curtain moved and Pan Xinbei walked right

in. "How could you be so spineless, teacher?" he asked. "The Japanese are at the gates, and you don't so much as fart. You're still just rattling on about 'freedom.' "

"Life is more trying than death now that everyone wants me dead," said He Wenjian.

"You could be our great hero if only you took the lead in resisting the Japanese," said Pan Xinbei. "At least that way you could die a glorious death."

He Wenjian stood up and slammed the table, roaring, "Scholars aren't meant to go to battle!"

Pan Xinbei remained obstinate. He walked over and slammed the table himself, "So then what are they good for?" he asked. "Waiting around till the time comes when they'll be bowing down to a portrait of the Japanese emperor three times a day? Is that it?"

"Scholars are meant to contribute to the enterprise of expounding upon the wisdom of the ancient sages, of the finer things in life," said He Wenjian. "And a foreign emperor couldn't get me to bow down so easily, either."

"You're all talk," said Pan Xinbei. "You're just a coward trying to save your own skin."

"You little rat!" He Wenjian cursed. "I'm just trying to stay alive. To hell with your goddamned bullshit."

Pan Xinbei reached the courtyard in a few short steps; then he turned around and cursed, "Fuck you, He! Just you wait."

A memory came to He Wenjian from when he was little—something that had to do with death, something he had almost forgotten over the course of all his romantic, carefree days.

One night, when he was five years old, he was being naughty with the servant girls and rushed clear out the gate. The winter night was so quiet he could almost hear the birds sleep-talking in their trees. Outside the gate, past the flagstone path and under the first quarter moon adorning the sky like a paper cut-out, the river noiselessly wound its way around the city. Then something, a spot, began to glitter in the river. The water's surface was catching the downy snow as it fell, like flowers whirling around in a kaleidoscope. This lonesome floating snow allured him, and he started slowly walking over with his hands stretched out, getting closer and closer, almost touching the snowflakes.

Ah Jin's father—the He family's devoted old servant—was the first one out the door. He had spotted He Wenjian in his cotton-padded jacket, floating in the river and spinning around like a pinwheel, grabbing with both hands at something in the sky. He took off his shoes and hurled them into the river, crying out: "Whichever evil spirit is responsible for this mess better beat it!"

After that incident, on the first snowfall of every year, He Wenjian's grandmother would take him to Murmur Temple on Big Dome Mountain. Grandmother and grandson would sit together on the snowy ground, reciting Buddhist scriptures, and praying for blessings and protection from calamities. They donated food and clothing to the temple, and gold-plating to refurbish the temple's Bodhisattva.

His grandmother died when he was ten years old. By then, his free, cheerful spirit had already taken a firm hold, and in those years he wouldn't go back to Murmur Temple no matter what.

He did go back though, later, when he heard about the special kind of bath they had there. Fields of wintersweet grew all over Big Dome Mountain, and every year, when the flowers bloomed, all the monks went to gather petals. The petals were mixed with mountain spring water that had never been exposed to sunlight, then compressed and sealed up in potted jars, which were subsequently buried in a mountain cave for a whole year. When it started getting cold, the mixture would be fetched and bathers could have a scoop ladled out into their bucket. After a bath like this, skin that had been dry and dull would come out glossy and smooth, and the delicious smell would linger for a few days without wearing off. So every year, once winter came, He Wenjian would go to the temple to take a wintersweet flower bath almost daily, bringing twice his normal offerings for the temple.

Today he thought about going to Murmur Temple—not for a bath, but to go pray to be blessed with survival.

Looking up, he couldn't see the sun for the dark clouds that covered the sky. A wind was slowly rising, and it looked like the first snowfall of the year was on its way. He put Ah Jin in charge of getting the family all packed up according to plan, and then he drove off alone to go look for Nora. He was leaving tomorrow, moving far away. It might even be their final goodbye. He wanted Nora to come with him to Murmur Temple.

Pan Xinbei was He Wenjian's best student, and Nora was his best girl.

His best girl—but not necessarily always by his side. They saw each other only when they felt like it. He had taken Nora under his wing the year that Pan Xinbei turned twenty-five, helping her to settle down in a little park called Cold Spice Gardens in Sanzhuangyuan Alley. Nora wasn't called Nora in those days; back then, she was Little Orchid Wang and she begged on the streets with her mother. She was six years old then; now she was sixteen.

As Nora was growing up in Cold Spice Gardens, He Wenjian would play the zither for her, and she would listen from dawn until dusk. They say the sound of the zither makes people noble, calming and steadying those who listen—and for five years, Nora listened quietly like a cold block of wood. Once she went a few days without saying so much as a few words, so He Wenjian was left with no choice but to change the music, putting on a Zhou Xuan song for her instead. Zhou Xuan was twelve years old back then, and had just released her first LP, "Special Express." It was an innocent yet flirtatious record, and Nora, who was around the same age as Zhou, took to it right away, adopting its innocence and flirtatiousness as her own.

There was another curious

episode, the time that Nora kept repeating some foul language she'd picked up from God knows where, in spite of the fact that she was always tucked away in her bedchamber. She went along happily dropping it into every sentence because she didn't realize it was obscene, like: "He Wenjian, is that you? I haven't seen you for fucking ages!"

Nora's mother explained that she had picked it up from the women who went past the back window selling fish. And truth be told, He Wenjian wasn't put off by it. In fact, in his heart of hearts, he actually approved of it. A beauty who doesn't curse is like a rose without thorns; when it comes right down to it, they're missing that spark of authenticity.

Anti-war leaflets fluttered all about on the empty street. Everything felt desolate.

When she saw him today, Nora said, "It's been a long time since you've been by. Does the sun rise in the west now, asshole?"

"There's no sun in the sky at all now," said He Wenjian. "It's overcast, and it might snow. Why don't you come with me to Murmur Temple to do a snowflake meditation?"

A few women were visible outside the window, peeking their heads over to look through. He Wenjian got suspicious and went out to take a look at the flock of women, but he didn't recognize a single one, and as soon as they saw him they scattered and hid.

He wanted to ask Nora about it, but she just grabbed hold of his sleeve, and, pulling him the whole way, thrust him out the door. "I'm leaving first thing tomorrow, too," she said. "I'm going with Old Liu, the head of Wuguo Film Studios. His wife died and now he wants to marry me. Those are his relatives who fled from Shanghai and Ningbo, they're staying here with me."

"There's no way I can take you with me," said He Wenjian, anxious. "It's out of my control and you know it."

"Why are you talking such nonsense?" said Nora, "Everybody has to run for their lives. I don't blame you, and you don't blame me. Every person has the freedom to live. So if I whore myself out to stay alive, you can't blame me for that either, dammit."

He Wenjian was leaning against the door with one foot inside and one foot outside. He sighed and said, "You've learned all my old tricks. I can't hold it against you without being a real hypocrite."

Nora slammed the door shut. Standing inside, she flaunted her soaring spirits by babbling on, letting loose a string of unprintable profanity.

He Wenjian stood outside, his mind running through a litany of old debts she owed to him. How much had he spent renovating Cold Spice Gardens? How much had he spent on all that furniture he'd bought for her? He'd raised her for ten years—how many tutors had he hired to teach her *guqin*, zither, calligraphy, painting, writing, and needlework... But soon he realized it wasn't really about the money. The real issue was that Nora was a virgin, and he still hadn't gotten to reap the benefits.

Yet another fine thing that the Japanese had ruined.

Forget it, he thought to himself, so long as I'm alive, there will always be fine things. I'm sure we'll meet again someday. And if Ibsen's Nora wouldn't stay, why should my Nora be any different?

He turned around to take another look at the door, still shut tight, and said, "Farewell, my little Nora!"

He saw the frigid street coming to life a little as a demonstration paraded by. The masses wanted to get together, to do something, to let off some steam. Rebellions, wars, parties and spectacles ... they're all just ways of letting off steam, and a demonstration at gunpoint ranks pretty highly in that regard,after all. You could read it all over each and every flushed face in the procession.

The demonstration marched past him, and one protester whispered to another, "Look, it's He Wenjian ... the deserter..." at which point a few words could be made out amid the buzz—*nationality, at stake, fate, battle, death before dishonor ...*

Then suddenly an ear-piercing voice rang out from the drone: "Brothers and sisters, step up! We must kill him to prevent his treason."

He Wenjian's hands trembled as he rushed to start the car. When he made it off the street, he was covered in sweat from head to toe, which made his desire to bathe in the wintersweet flowers at Murmur Temple that much stronger. Going around a corner, he turned to look back and saw that the street behind him was completely deserted—there wasn't a soul in sight. He couldn't help but think that in the long rivers of history, he was no more than a purposeless nobody who wouldn't hurt a fly. How could anyone make such a big fuss over taking his life? He had a sneaking suspicion that everything he had just witnessed had been a hallucination.

Two little monks—Jihuan and Jixing—were carrying water and playing by the riverside in front of Murmur Temple. They giggled as they teased the ants on the ground with cogon grass.

Jihuan saw He Wenjian walk by and said, "What a coincidence you're here, Master He! The wintersweet flowers were just collected the day before yesterday. They dried in the sun and then soaked in spring water all of last night. The oil seeped out from the flowers already, but it hasn't been stored away in the cave yet, so you're just in time to have yourself a nice fresh flower oil bath."

"You two little masters are sure in good spirits," said He Wenjian, "We're about to be up to our necks in enemy fire, and you're still here playing with ants?"

"Well you must be in a good mood yourself," said Jixing. "We're already up to our behinds in enemy fire, and you're coming up the mountain for a flower bath."

Jihuan gave Jixing a little shove and dropped the cogon grass he'd been holding. "We heard a few days ago that the Japanese don't destroy temples, so we've all calmed down a bit and are having some fun. If Mr. He wants to take a flower bath, then we'll just carry a little extra water."

Bei Yue, the Head Monk of Murmur Temple, and Master Yin Guang from Quick Rock Mountain, saw quite a lot of each other. Once, Master Yin Guang wrote the character "Death" and hung it up in his bedroom. He wrote another "Death" for Bei Yue, who hung it up in the study next to his bedroom.

Incense burned thick at Murmur Temple. The people of Wuguo all said Bei Yue was a medium, half-immortal.

When Bei Yue and He Wenjian saw each other, they went off to the study to moisten and grind their ink stick and wrote, reliving the scene of their very first encounter. He Wenjian had just turned five at the time, and Bei Yue remembered everything about him with perfect clarity—everything he wore, and every word he said. He had taken down the "Death" character Yin Guang had written, and wrote a giant "Life" to hang in its place. Bei Yue didn't object, either; he just smiled.

They had a very peculiar relationship: He Wenjian took Bei Yue as a father, since his own had died prematurely. But he didn't respect him—he would curse and lose his temper any time he felt like it. One time, when he had been bullied in town, he went up the mountain to take it out on Bei Yue. He picked up a book of scriptures and smashed it on Bei Yue's bald head, leaving him with a bump. But still, Bei Yue went on smiling. In class, He Wenjian would tell the students that he only felt completely free when he was with Bei Yue, and that he hoped to die of old age right there at Murmur Temple.

"I want to live, but it's all so hard," said He Wenjian.

He dropped his writing brush and kneeled at Bei Yue's feet, saying, "Deep down, I am afraid. I've had a tightness in my chest the past few days, like I'm not getting enough air. When I walk, my feet float, as though I were treading on cotton."

Bei Yue just went on writing characters, without helping him up. He said, "This world is all a fantasy land. Life and death are nothing more than fate toying with people. In fact, there is no such thing as life and death in this world—life is death, and death is life. Without fully grasping the essence of the two, you will live your whole life in anguish."

He Wenjian stood up furiously and pointed at him, "You're still going on with all your empty talk at a time like this? Fine, go right ahead and die then. Are you really prepared to depart?"

Bei Yue started to laugh.

Jihuan walked in and asked, "Which would Mr. He like to do first? Eat, or take a bath?"

"I'll take a bath first," said He Wenjian. "Throw in a little extra wintersweet oil for me."

He looked up and saw a few scattered snowflakes floating in the sky outside. Their gentle falling was unbelievably slow, as though they were yearning for the sky, unable to bear this separation. Just one look, and tears welled up in He Wenjian's eyes. "First I'm going to go sit a while on the snowy ground and recite The Great Compassion Mantra. I'll take my bath when I'm finished," he said. "I just realized I never ate lunch, and I'm still not even hungry. Just like a wandering soul. A person who can't even tell when he's hungry has lost at least half of his joy in life."

A woman passed by outside the window, and He Wenjian called out to her without a second thought, "Nora, come in quick. It's cold outside."

"There's no one out there," said Jihuan.

He Wenjian pushed open the window to look. Sure enough, there was nobody walking by. "I've been really exhausted the past two days," he said, laughing.

Bei Yue was still writing characters. He spoke without looking up, "Go read the Heart Sutra. Reading it without stopping will calm you down. You'll feel better as soon as you let go."

Jihuan carried a praying mat in one hand, and offered his other to He Wenjian, helping him to sit down on a boulder to the east of the temple. "Come back in if it starts snowing heavily, Mr. He," he said.

The snow never came down too heavily, but it came without stopping—falling sparsely to the ground in a languid, decadent drifting. He Wenjian closed his eyes as teardrops gathered in their corners, and began to recite the Heart Sutra. His nostrils were assailed by the fragrance of plum, and the ground stretched out in a vast expanse below the silent sky. Chanting the sutra, he trembled as he fathomed the depths of his fear of death.

Gunshots echoed out from down the mountain. Refugees arrived and crowded into the temple with children and elders in tow. Candlelight filled the temple rooms as the densely packed queue made its way up the mountain, completely vulnerable and defenseless, seeking a divine protection that could not be seen.

On the boulder, He Wenjian sat in quiet meditation without moving a muscle. His breathing was weak and he was deaf to the sounds of gunshots and people. Without his noticing, the sutra on his lips had transformed into a couple lines of romantic poetry by Liu Yong and Du Mu that he had always been keen on in peacetimes. He cherished their poetry with all his heart, and at a time like this he felt himself fusing with their words.

Time passed without his awareness. Most of the candles in the temple had gone out one by one, and there was nobody coming up the mountain on the little stone path. The snow was piling up on the ground. Then, in the stillness, the glimmer of a candle appeared, making its way through the snow. It was Jihuan and Jixing. They walked over and pushed He Wenjian down to the ground, then carried him over to the bath area.

He Wenjian had been sitting out there for a long time. His body was rigid and he couldn't speak as his head lay cocked to one side, eyes on the floor. The light from the candle shone upon all sorts of junk along the way—a young child's cloth shoe, a woman's headband, a carrying pole, leggings, a shattered bowl, an elementary school primer... It was all too pitiful for words. He Wenjian sighed. He didn't like looking at these things. He was born with eyes meant for beauty alone.

The bath was piping hot, and the candle was burning brightly. The two boys hoisted him up and plopped him into the bucket, and in the delicious hot water, He Wenjian warmed up in no time. But while his body softened, he still couldn't say a word.

Monk Bei Yue walked in. "In your bid for survival, you almost froze yourself to death," he said, laughing. "But seeing as you're so dedicated, how would you like it if I sealed up your fleshly spirit and immortal soul until safer, more peaceful times? Then you'll just wake up automatically."

It's true what they say, thought He Wenjian, he really does have great magical powers. From his wooden tub, He Wenjian expressed his enthusiasm by nodding over and over.

A sudden transformation came over Bei Yue's face, which locked into a cold stare. He pointed at He Wenjian, who immediately fell asleep in a daze. He slept through the whole land being torn to pieces, in a darkness that neither sun nor moon could penetrate, unaware of the shuttling of time or the turning of the cosmos. Then he woke up, just like Bei Yue had planned: eight years had passed and things were calm now, the sun was shining once more. At the temple, there wasn't a soul in sight. The walls of the bathing room had collapsed, weeds were growing all over outside, and a pine tree had sprouted out from the wooden tub in which he'd been slumbering. For a while he listened to the great clamor of gongs and drums coming from down the mountain, which let him know that the war of resistance against Japan had been victorious, and the people were celebrating.

He Wenjian was at once startled and happy. He had avoided disaster, and from this point forward he could go back to enjoying all the boundless romance that this lovely strip of earth had to offer. Lips wiggling, he practiced speaking, "I ... I ... love ... life!"

Then a slender fellow with a full beard appeared outside the door. He walked in with long strides, carrying a gun over his shoulder and a machete in his hand. Standing next to the tub, he glared at He Wenjian, indignant and stunned. "I searched high and low for you, and after all that you were hiding right here?"

He Wenjian recognized him. It was Pan Xinbei.

Without saying another word, Pan Xinbei brandished his machete and struck. In the shivering gale of the impending blade, He Wenjian cried out his last words, "I want to live! Is that so much to ask?"

There was no light in the darkness of the black vault of heaven. Then, the strike of a match shone bright, igniting a half-used candle. "Here in the mountains, the draft always messes with the candles and puts them out," said Jihuan. "Are you awake, Mr. He? Time to get up and eat. Jixing, go ahead to the kitchen and warm up some food."

He Wenjian opened his eyes and looked around—there was no Bei Yue, no gongs or drums sounding out down the mountain, and definitely no machete-wielding Pan Xinbei.

"Can you talk, Mr. He? Now that you've had your soak in the flower bath?" asked Jihuan, concerned. "Please, say something."

"I want to live," said He Wenjian. "Is that so much to ask?"

2015

Mount Xianglu

Ye Mi / 叶 弥
Translated by Natascha Bruce

After moving to Huamatou[1], a town in Baiju Bay, I made a steady stream of friends: Old Wu, the gatekeeper at the big Daoist temple; Jimmy Jiang, the traveller; Hua Ya; little Tiger Zhang and his mother; Lu Lan and her father, Old Lu; Luo Hanfang.

Then, for about six months, I made no friends at all. There was a murder, is why. A reclusive local woman was killed in the night by her live-in boyfriend. They were unmarried but living together and, according to the townsfolk, she got what she deserved. She'd invited the wolf into her own house, they said—if that wasn't asking for it, what was? I was fit and healthy; always in for a dare. But, even so, I found myself becoming more cautious after the incident. I stopped walking alone at night and avoided meeting new people. I didn't want to give anyone cause to say I'd been asking for it.

One particular day, it drizzled constantly until evening, when it stopped. Standing by the loofah gourd trellis to the west of my house, I could see Mount Xianglu in the north, emitting pretty white trails of mist, soft as muslin. Clouds drifted overhead like streaks of fine white sand and, behind them, the sky turned from pale blue to purple.

There was something special about the moon, too: a powder-pink crescent, clear and elegant. The day's rain had rinsed away any coquettish or irritable humour, leaving it to radiate a charming, innocent beauty.

I'd never seen such a moon before, and felt reluctant to go back inside. When something's extremely beautiful, people in Huamatou say it's "handsome." Not pretty, not beautiful—but *handsome*.

I'd climb the peak to see this handsome moon, I decided; that would surely be fun. I put on some comfortable sandals and a baggy skirt, and picked up half a bag of sunflower seeds, which I ate as I walked, looking up at the moon. The road I walked along was named Huidao Road, and did not yet have street lights. During the day, people rode up and down it on the No. 600 bus. There was no nightlife out there in the sticks, so by the time I set out, the road was deserted. It stretched blankly ahead, wide, flat, and misty; I could have walked it with my eyes closed.

One road, one person, one moon. There were rice paddies either side, where fireflies flitted back and forth but never settled, their lights still dim. The paddies stretched as far as the eye could see and, in dotted clusters, frogs croaked at the top of their lungs. Nature's like that; you can't let it vex you.

A contented, cheering walk, and yet still I noted signs of danger: on the damp ground at the edge of the road lay a single, tawny-yellow butterfly wing, criss-crossed with wavy lines in coffee-brown and black. It was only slightly smaller than a sparrow wing. My heart pounded and then, a few paces later, did so once again: this time, there was a pair of wings. By the looks of it, they'd been torn from the body of the same butterfly. For some reason, this made me think of the murdered woman from the town, and how the man who killed her said he never intended to do it; he'd been feeling a bit down that day, and he hated that she talked so much, so he'd squeezed her throat. Squeezed until she had no breath left. She died, and at first he was delighted, then a little later he felt scared. And grief... well, that came even later.

A similar mood had probably led someone to pull the wings off a butterfly. Maybe they didn't plan to kill it, they were just seeking a few moments of pleasure.

But what kind of person would find pleasure in that?

Not a child, I hoped!

I picked up the pair of wings, and walked back to collect the first one. To prevent them being trampled by other passers-by, I used a stick to dig a tiny hole in the slope at the side of the road, and buried them.

Suddenly, I heard a voice behind me: 'Isn't there a tangerine tree just over there? Why not bury them under that?'

I looked ahead and saw it was true, there was a tangerine tree, laden with little fruits. In my fear and sadness, I'd somehow failed to spot it. I glanced behind at the speaker, who turned out to be a young man dressed in a white shirt and jeans. He cut a dashing figure; his body seemed a series of finely-chiselled lines. As I looked, I felt an involuntary flicker of appreciation. The temperature had cooled to a pleasant chill but he carried a palm-leaf fan, which gave him an affected, bohemian air.

A flicker of appreciation, that was all. Huamatou was full of boys like this. They were clever. One glance and they had you sussed, could tell who you were and the kind of family you came from. And they were only interested in girls from the well-off kinds of family. Those were the girls they wanted to date—to parade around as their sisters or their mothers, as a flimsy mask for what was really going on. That's what happened with the murdered woman: she met her killer on the street, let him act like her little brother, then invited him to move in.

In this world, a butterfly has to watch out for its wings, and a woman for her throat. My wariness and resentment must have shown in my face, because the boy looked suddenly uncomfortable. He spun around, marched down the slope, and set off towards the tiny villages in the north.

After composing myself,

I decided to continue. I was shaken, but didn't want to give in.

He was walking the way I'd planned to go; Mount Xianglu was at the northern end of Huidao Road. I didn't want to follow him, because I didn't want him to see me and try to make conversation again. It wouldn't be the first time that kind of thing had happened—when strange men take a liking to you, they'll try a thousand different ways to get you talking. I decided to head west, then find a smaller road to take me north again.

I walked until I reached the shores of Blue Lake. The lake has been developed well, in a way that retains the charm of days gone by, although it is no longer home to the rare creatures and magical plants recorded in history books, much less surrounded by its legendary circle of weathered rock. But as a person of my times, I've learned to appreciate things as they are. Blue Lake is shrinking. In years to come, there may well be no water left at all.

Such fears have become an accepted part of our lives, and so I say to you: my happy outlook is a conscious choice, and it's my most precious resource. While humans are fretting over the end of days, I try to savour the present moment, storing joyful memories for the future.

I found a grassy path heading east from the lake. I'd walked some way past the mountain, and now needed to walk back, looking for a connecting path north.

The sky went from blue to purple, then purple to charcoal grey; soon it would fade to black. Night was closing in. The moon glowed like a precious gemstone against the darkening sky, too delicate to illuminate my way. It was half-past seven, meaning I had at least three hours before the light faded completely. Plenty of time; there was no need to worry.

I'd never ventured into the outlying villages before. Whenever I'd caught sight of their blurry outlines from Huidao Road, they'd seemed to me very simply arranged—identical little houses, fields of rice and vegetables, trees of all sizes: willow, camphor, gingko, magnolia. That night, I realised how wrong I'd been. They were tangled, intricate mazes. Roads crossed, one village merged into another, and nowhere was there anything so civilised as a street sign. Instead, they were full of secret signs only other villagers could know: turn the corner at the house with the gingko tree and you'll get to the main road; pass the house with the crumbling earth wall and you'll get to the little footbridge across the river; cross that particular part of the bamboo grove and you'll arrive in the next village over. The villages were like kaleidoscopes; one careless nudge and everything looked different. Or like a Rubik's Cube, where you made one mistake and the whole thing was wrong. You overlooked the little log bridge at your peril—a short, coarsely-cut length of willow laid across the brook, one end behind Old Jin's house, the other leading to the back of Old Wang's. And if you crossed the bridge from Old Jin's to Old Wang's, then you'd be able to cross from the south of the village to the north, and that was where you'd find the little path that led to the foot of Mount Xianglu.

Very quickly, I became hopelessly, unexpectedly lost. There were some houses that I kept seeing, over and over again, while some of the roads were frighteningly empty and unfamiliar. I realised I was walking in circles through the same few villages, without coming any closer to finding a way out. I knocked on six doors asking for directions, but every new set of instructions was as complicated as the last. I walked and walked, but only felt more lost. The villagers were cold and suspicious. When they opened their doors to me, they always cast an eye over my shoulder before answering, as though checking for undesirable characters lurking in the background. Finally, at my wits end, I knocked on the door of a middle-aged woman and said, "I'm from Huamatou. I'll pay you one hundred *kuai* to take me up the peak."

The woman slowly extended

her hand.

"Sure," she said. "Show me the money."

I dug deep into the pockets of my skirt, but all I had was some sunflower seeds and the keys to my house.

"If you don't have the money, you can leave your phone here as a deposit," said the woman.

At which I could only force a smile. I was a pleasure-seeker; I didn't carry a phone with me while I was out enjoying myself. This woman didn't seem like the callous, calculating type—she had an honest, sun-baked face, and her voice was low and quavering. There was an unnatural tremor to her outstretched hand, as though she were ashamed. But when she spoke again, her tone was steely: "Who's going to trust you, if you've got nothing to show for yourself? No one, you'll see."

Is that all trust is, I thought to myself—a mobile phone or one hundred *kuai*?

She shut the door.

The problem then was that I couldn't find the path to the mountain, but neither did I know the way back to Huidao Road, which would have taken me home. I was trapped in a maze of villages, and felt profoundly confused: weren't the villagers of Baiju Bay supposed to be warm and honest? Who had told me that? My grandmother, I remembered. And my mother, too. But now it was my turn, would I be able to say the same?

If I hadn't lost my way, it would have been a wonderful occasion for enjoying myself. I was so anxious that the surroundings flitted by like clouds. Now, however, after all this time, I can describe to you the beauty of those villages. For they were truly beautiful, each one nestled in trees, their gravel roads neat and gleaming. Limpid streams wound their way around every household, filled with shoals of tiny fish, burbling into the night air. Wild chrysanthemums sprang up all over, and bamboo groves swayed with the breeze. Industrious farmers kept every plot like a tidy woman keeps her bed, with the edges neat and the corners sharp. There wasn't a weed to be seen.

I looked up at the moon, which was edging towards the west. Judging by its position, it must have been about ten o'clock. I'd been lost for over two hours.

Suddenly, my ears pricked: I could hear someone singing. It was a man's voice, and he was heading towards me. I gripped a sunflower seed, and made a bet with myself: if I threw it and it landed on my head, he was good news; if it landed on the ground, he was not. I threw it towards my head, and it landed squarely on top. Good luck was on its way! I stood there with the seed still on my head, smiling in the direction of the singing man.

He came closer, then stopped. Clearly, he could tell I wasn't a villager, and had guessed my predicament. He waited for me to speak. I said, "Excuse me..."

But after those two words, I couldn't say anything else. I realised he was the boy I'd met on Huidao Road, and refused to talk to. I didn't entirely trust him. He was still holding his palm leaf fan.

In that moment, he recognised me, too, standing mutely before him. We stayed awkwardly facing one another.

It was he who broke the silence: "What's up?"

There was no harshness to his tone; he didn't seem to mind about what had happened on Huidao Road. My heart was racing, but I knew better than to show it; he might be the only person who could help me find my way.

"I'm lost," I said, casually. "No doubt that happens to strangers all the time round here?"

He laughed, an easy, fitting laugh, then said, confidently, "Well, you're lucky to run into me. I know all the roads round here."

I appreciated his confidence, although that alone was no guarantee.

I decided not to go home, but to keep on with my original plan. It was a little risky, and this unexpected new guide of mine only added to the danger. I followed as he led the way, asking his name and surname.

"I'm from Su village," he

said, an air of mystery to his tone. "My surname's Su."

He didn't ask for mine, which I found slightly strange.

I took precautions: under the cover of darkness, I secretly picked up a small brick, and said to him that I had to call my husband. Turning so that I was out of his line of vision, I spoke loudly into the brick—"Go ahead and sleep," I yelled. "I'm still out climbing Mount Xianglu, to look at the moon... Don't worry, I'm with young Su here, from Su Village, he's strong and capable..."

Slipping the brick into my pocket, I turned back to Su.

"Su," I said, "it's been a miserable day. People kept turning me away, no one wanted to help. Some wanted money, others were just icy-cold, as though we were worlds apart."

"You were unlucky," he said, placidly. "If you'd met my girl Swallow or my old godma, you'd have been up the peak in no time."

We passed through one village after another. I was still nervous, but he kept up a gentle chatter, telling me secrets about each one we passed.

"This magnolia's been in Old Ye's family for a hundred years. It blossoms at the start of summer, half white, half purple. It's not a graft—it just grows that way. We call it the husband and wife tree."

A tremor of unease: was he insinuating something?

Then: "You see the bottle gourds at the entrance to this house? At the market, they fetch double the price of other people's, because they're joined at the top. That's a rare sight."

Another tremor: conjoined gourds? A hint?

He stopped behind a brick and wood house, pointing at it with the handle of his fan. Lowering his voice to a mysterious whisper, he asked, "Have you got guts? Tell the truth: yes or no?"

I made a rapid calculation in my head. Then replied, "Yes. I do Taekwondo. I can fight off two men with my bare hands."

He seemed a little disappointed, and his interest abruptly waned. It was exactly the effect I'd been hoping for.

"But why won't you tell

me," I pressed him, suddenly enthusiastic. "Come on, tell me!"

He sighed, then told the story as we walked, without once looking back at me.

"The grandpa from this family married his first wife when he was eighteen. His bride was the daughter of one of the big families from the town, very beautiful—as beautiful as you. On the wedding night, he got up to go to the toilet, and saw his new wife combing her hair by the light of the moon. Her long, long hair, which fell from the dressing table all the way to the floor... Only it turned out that she'd taken her head off and put it on the table. She was a fox spirit, an enchanted, beautiful fox-woman."

This time, I was almost sure he was flirting with me. No man had ever compared me to a beautiful fox-spirit; no man would dare.

I ignored it, and urged him to hurry up. I wasn't worried he'd try anything—I'd given my "husband" a "call", after all, and he would be too scared of the potential consequences.

We emerged from the maze of villages, arriving at a path that led straight to the mountain. Low carpets of wild chrysanthemums grew either side, stretching all the way to the horizon.

Relaxing a little, I asked, "So you still have a godmother? And who's this Swallow girl you mentioned?"

I knew the way from there, and we would soon be parting ways. The mountain was at the northern end of the chrysanthemum path, and Huidao Road was to the south. I waited politely for his reply, planning to say goodbye once he'd finished.

But, rather than answering my question, he surprised me by saying, "Seeing as I've brought you here, it's only fair that you accompany me to that village up ahead. It's on your way. I'm going to visit my godma."

He pointed to the village in question, which lay at the foot of the mountain; unavoidably on my way. In one of the houses, there was a faint glimmer of lamplight.

"I can't," I replied. "I'm going up the peak to see the

moon. Look, you can see it's about to sink below the horizon."

"True," he said. "It's about to sink, and you're not even at the viewing platform halfway up. You won't catch it now, so you might as well come with me."

He had a point. I'd been wandering about for more than three hours, and couldn't quite face the prospect of heading home yet. Perhaps he could sense my mood, although it had nothing to do with him or his idea of what was fair. Keeping my face stern, I asked, "Is there anything interesting in the village? Conjoined gourds or two-tone magnolias, perhaps?"

My haughty tone did nothing to dispel his enthusiasm; he was almost impatient.

"Of course," he said, "loads of fun things! Follow me!'

He walked a few paces, then noticed I hadn't moved. "Hurry!" he urged, stamping his foot. "Didn't you hear that there'll be a magic lamp on Mount Xianglu tonight? Let's go ask my godma, she'll know when to look for it."

All too often, I find my curiosity overcomes my reason, like I'm a cat. And thus, off I went with Su. A magic lamp? On Mount Xianglu? I'd never heard of it before. Surely I would have, if it really existed? But maybe, I thought, people nowadays deliberately ignore that kind of news, because all they care about are murder stories, and things like that. Or maybe it was a closely-guarded village secret—something only villagers knew, that you could only hear about by word of mouth.

How many secrets were lurking in these unassuming little villages? Did the country roads turn into an enchanted labyrinth after dark?

Su's godmother was called Granny Xia. The house with the glimmer of light at the entrance to the village turned out to be a little earthen chapel. It was almost eleven when we arrived, a time when most villagers were usually tucked up in bed, but there was quite a crowd praying in the chapel.

Su took me inside. Everyone was kneeling, and he knelt, too. I stood stiffly at the back and he pulled at me, trying to make me kneel with them. It annoyed me. I told him I wasn't religious. He said that he wasn't either, but non-believers could still show the gods a little respect, couldn't they? I had no reason to trust him—I knelt for a few seconds, then ran outside. There was something too intimate about the way he had pulled me down, and I wanted to establish some distance between us.

A while later, he emerged from the chapel with Granny Xia, and they came to stand beside me, chatting.

"Did you walk over? Is Swallow any better?" Granny Xia asked Su, her face creased with wrinkles. Her skin resembled a shrivelled leaf but she had twinkly eyes, which made her look meek and affectionate.

"A bit better," he replied. "I've just been to see her. I haven't been for a week, and she was worrying herself sick, thinking I'd found someone else. But she's better now I've talked to her."

"Well, are you looking for someone else?"

"Maybe," laughed Su. I could hear he was joking, but then he winked at me, which made me angry all over again. Damn him! He really was shameless.

"And how's her flock of red-rumped swallows?"

"Oh, they're happy as can be. Much happier than her."

"And your Ma?" Granny Xia changed the subject.

"Ma's doing better than she was in the autumn. Always worrying about Long Life. She's the one who sent me over tonight, saying I could ask about Long Life while I was here. It was still early, so I went to Swallow's house first, but she kept me longer than expected. So that's why I'm late."

"Long Life's fine," said Granny Xia. "Gets up at the crack of dawn every morning, runs about all over the place. She's got a terrible temper on her! Full of fire, that one—enormous appetite, eats everything. I mean it, everything! She smashed a little vase of mine the other day, so I chased her around and gave her a few good whacks. That kept her in line for a few hours... "

She laughed, and so did Su. They were cheerful like that, but I didn't share their mood. This so-called "Swallow" was Su's wife, I presumed, and if he had a wife, then what was he doing flirting with strange women like me?

It was eleven o'clock. My earlier fears lingered, overlaid with resentment for Su. I considered going home.

I coughed.

Immediately, Su said to Granny Xia, "I heard the magic lamp will be on the peak tonight. What do your calculations say, when will it be out?"

She glanced shrewdly in my direction.

"Oh, I'm too old for those kinds of calculations..." she said, haltingly. "I haven't got it right for years, no one trusts me anymore. Yesterday, I calculated that it'd be there today at a quarter past midnight...but who knows? Who knows if it'll be there or not? *Aiyo*, these days the climate's changing, and the lamps don't come when they should."

This Granny Xia, blaming her miscalculations on climate change!

The pair of them discussed the magic lamp with the utmost gravity. It didn't seem like a trap—I felt at least eighty percent sure of my safety. I hesitated for a moment, then decided not to question how reliable that assessment really was: I would go to the peak to find out.

"So is Swallow your wife?" I asked Su, when we were back on the path.

"Pretty much. But we don't have a marriage certificate yet," he replied.

"A man must take responsibility for his woman, whether the marriage is official or not," I said, earnestly. Once I'd said it, the sentence buzzed in my ears, and I was silent for a while. When had I become so feeble? Where had I learnt to say this stuff?

"Who's Long Life?" I asked.

Su burst out laughing. A full, hearty laugh; he really did seem to be a cheerful person.

"Long Life's a hen," he said.

Then he told me the story:

Long Life was a hen, and they kept her so she'd bring long life to Su's mother. Hence the name. Three years earlier, Su's mother had contracted a strange illness, which made her throw up anything she ate. Even the big hospital couldn't cure her. When it seemed that any breath might be her last, Su's father paid a visit to the big Doaist temple in Huamatou, intending to ask the oracle for help. He arrived late, and there were no priests to be seen. But Old Wu, the gatekeeper, listened to his predicament and suggested that keeping a long life hen might work. That's what people did in the old days. A cockerel for men, a hen for women. You had to look after the bird with the utmost care, because if it died, so did the person. And if the bird lived, the person lived. So Su's father went to the Huamatou market and bought a sturdy little hen, which he left with Granny Xia. Since then, the vomiting sickness had disappeared, and Su's mother was still alive.

By the end of this charming tale of village life, my nerves were settled: these were kind-hearted people indeed!

...but hadn't everyone in the town said the same thing about the murderer? That he was always grinning, used to hug the Lin baby in the grocery store? Kiss him, even.

Two days before, I'd read a story about Chu Minyi, the man found guilty of treason for his association with the Japanese collaborator, Wang Jingwei. On the day he was taken out to the city execution ground, to be shot by the Nationalist forces, he told journalists that his body was in fine shape, and they should give it to the hospital for dissection, so that his bones and organs could be used for medical research. People have so many sides to them! In the dead of night, in that desolate spot, I had to be especially careful.

I couldn't help feeling a twinge of regret. I'm a woman, and I know well my feminine weaknesses; regret is one. But we'd reached the foot of the mountain, and there was no time for such thoughts.

Once again, Su struck me as a little strange. He could see everything, despite the dark:

the little egrets hiding silently in the marsh, the pheasants in the bamboo grove, the frogs beneath the wild amaranth. He even claimed to spot a wild orchid, five or six paces away. He listed everything he could see in great detail; at one point, sensing my disbelief, he threw a stone into the bamboo grove and, sure enough, up rose a startled pheasant. But, even so, I refused to believe him about the orchid. We made a bet about who was right—we bet a hug. My curiosity got the better of my caution, and I gladly accepted the challenge. Together, we walked along the edge of the road, where Su switched on his flashlight: there really was an orchid. Then we walked back again, but he made no mention of the hug. Which was tactful of him.

I couldn't see any of the things he saw in the dark and, inwardly, I envied him.

Are you a ghost? I asked him, in my head. But of course he wasn't; the night was making me confused. Anyway, there was no right answer—I was afraid of him as a man or as a ghost. The magic lamp was scary, too. Perhaps it was an evil omen. Perhaps it would rise up and, quick as a flash, Su would turn into a ghost?

"Did...did you ever see a magic lamp before?" I asked him, stammering nervously.

"Only once, when I was eight. Granny Xia took me up the mountain to see it."

"What was it like?"

"A tiny flame, surrounded by a glowing halo," he replied. "It wobbled up from somewhere at the bottom of the mountain, and when it was almost halfway up, it disappeared. I saw six of them, all exactly the same. I imagined fairies carrying them up, then blowing them out."

It was a gripping story. Whether it was true or not, after I'd heard it, my thoughts stopped running away with themselves. I had to admit, there were some truly delightful things in this world, and sometimes even just thinking about them was a powerful comfort.

We reached the viewing platform and, all of a sudden, the sliver of moon was nowhere to be seen. With it gone, the quiet that surrounded us felt even thicker; there wasn't the faintest breath of wind. Viewed from halfway up the peak, the ground below was like a huge, ink-black river. After watching for a long time, I had the sensation that my feet were floating above the ground and my soul was departing my body. Su sat down beside me—sat very close, and as he sat, I heard him sigh with contentment. This wasn't subtle at all; it was brazen as could be. He picked a blade of foxtail grass, humming softly. From the looks of it, he was really enjoying all this. There were twenty minutes before the lamp was due to appear, and I needed them to pass safely.

"Are you humming the song you were singing when we met?" I asked.

"Yeah," he said. "*One key for one lock, he's the key, she's the lock...*"

He would have carried on singing, but I interrupted: "Did you really go and see Swallow? Your godmother said she has a flock of red-rumped swallows."

I could see him smiling through the flagging moonlight. His tone, too, was smiley: "Hey, she's...special."

"Special" meant eccentric; it was what people in those parts said when someone was different in some way.

"...she's quite something. People like her usually stay in the city, but she came back here after teacher-training college, to be a primary school teacher. She teaches everything—language, maths, sports... First, because she loves children; second, because of the swallows. Why swallows, you ask? Well, there are more than a hundred, and they live in a wooden hut on the hill behind the school. She's always taking the kids there to feed them, and the swallows are always coming to see her in the classroom while she's teaching. So that's why everyone calls her Swallow, or Swallow Girl. Her real name's Qi Ah-Qiao. I asked her, I said, *Qi Ah-Qiao, you think people are going to be calling you Swallow Girl, even when you're sixty?*"

"Well, she sounds like a good one, you should treat her well. Hurry up and marry her, give her some peace of mind." I couldn't pass up an opportunity to nag him.

"You're right," he said. "You know, I had so many offers to get out of here and make something of myself, but she wouldn't let me. So I stayed."

"Why wouldn't she let you?" I asked. This was my first genuine spark of interest.

"She was afraid I'd cheat.... Women are all like that. And, the way I am, I didn't really mind either way. I can be happy wherever I am."

"How come?" I couldn't help asking. He didn't seem to have thought about it before. He pondered carefully for a moment, then gave me his reason: "I can sing love songs anywhere!"

My first instinct was to laugh. Then I thought it over, and realised it made sense.

Twenty minutes had passed, but there weren't any magic lamps floating up from the bottom of the mountain. I said we should wait a bit longer, and suggested Su sing us a song. A little bashful, he walked to the edge of the viewing platform, where he crouched with his back to me, looking down. He sang: "*One key for one lock, he's the key, she's the lock. The water's clear, the river's long, he's the oar and she's the boat. In spring the hills ring with birdsong, in fall they're red with maple.*"

He dragged the song out, but even when he'd finished, there was still no lamp. He started on a second one. When he finished that one, I stood up and headed for the path back down.

"Wait a bit more!" he said, chasing after. "I've got a belly full of love songs, I could sing till dawn!"

I didn't answer. The walk down was quick, and I arrived on a path that led straight to Huidao road. Su followed. I knew the way from there, so I sped up.

"Thank you for your help, but now you can go home," I said to him as I walked. "I need to hurry, my husband will be worried."

"No need to thank me," he said. "I have to take Huidao Road, too—I live at the south end."

I kept up my pace. Su stayed close enough behind that I could see him when I turned. I was panting, while he was still singing in the same cheery, leisurely manner. When we were almost at Huidao Road, he stopped and ran towards me, coming so close that I could almost feel his breath. I spun around.

"What do you think you're doing?" I snapped.

The nearby leaves shuddered in alarm.

"I wanted to escort you home," he said, apologetically.

I glanced down the road. I'd never heard of anything happening to anyone while walking along it.

"There's no need," I said, softening my tone. "This road is perfectly safe."

The only unsafe thing about it is you, I added, silently.

"It's not about safety," he said.

"Then what is it about?"

"A man's honour."

That was quite clearly not the reason. But, after some thought, I decided to respect it, all the same.

I walked as quickly as before, and Su lagged behind. Then, a while later, he ran up and presented me with an enormous ear of rice—it must have weighed about a pound. To tell the truth, I'd never seen such a big one in all my life. It was beautifully proportioned, and smelled wonderful. Before I'd even finished exclaiming, Su produced wild chrysanthemums—yellow, and slightly damp with dew. They were glossy and substantial, and their leafy stems bunched in my hands. I gasped with delight, feeling the tension inside me relax. It had been so long since I'd felt such joy!

I held the rice ear and the flowers together. The combination was surprisingly harmonious, for two plants with so little in common.

Su beamed, loudly proclaiming: "Thank the heavens, thank the earth! Finally, you're happy!"

"Thank *you*," I replied, genuinely touched. I'd spent four hours with him, and that was the first truly sincere thing I had said.

There were lights on in Huamatou, and I could see where I lived. I stopped, intending to say goodbye.

"Really, it's me that should be thanking you," said Su. "I saw you for the first time last summer, down by Blue Lake. You were wearing a green skirt, like a fairy. Then when I saw you burying the butterfly wings earlier, I thought to myself: she really is a fairy. People always say bookish women aren't beautiful, but you're an exception...so I wanted to talk to you, and my wish came true. The pleasure's all mine!"

He sounded a little unsure of himself. Not a lot, but enough to tell me that his infatuation was making him nervous.

Had he really been secretly aware of my existence for all this time?

"Good bye, Teacher Ai Wosu," he said mischievously, as he walked off. In the distance, I watched him start skipping cheerfully along the road, brandishing his fan. God, I thought, realising I was seeing through the darkness, had I acquired my night vision from him?

He knew my name. He knew who I was. But I knew nothing about him. He probably knew all sorts of things about me, like that I taught in a university, wrote poems and fairy tales, that I was unmarried and had a hot temper...that I lived in a little neighbourhood at the back of Huamatou.

And then there was that brick telephone, which I'd used to call my imaginary husband...

He must have seen straight through that little act.

He was a cheerful person; he wasn't agonising over these tiny details. His wish had come true, and he was happy. And me? How would I rate my evening? He'd felt love, while I'd been mired in fear and resentment. I'd always considered myself a pleasure-seeker, someone who knew how to enjoy life, but I'd just passed up an opportunity for happiness, for no real reason at all.

I was a cheerful person, I decided. I would enjoy what was left of the evening.

Back home, I prepared myself a welcome feast. I set three wine cups on the ceramic-topped table in my yard, one for heaven and earth, one for Su, and one for myself. Shaoxing rice wine was 5.2

kuai per half-litre from the Lin Grocery Store—cheap and delicious, with a crisp, refined taste. I placed the rice ear and chrysanthemums that Su had given me in the middle of the table. In the weak light of approaching dawn, there was an unexpected symmetry to their beauty. When I thought back over the evening, I felt as if a gentle breeze were caressing my body: the pink crescent of the waxing moon, the beautiful maze of villages, Su's songs and stories, the little village chapel, Granny Xia and Swallow, Long Life the hen, the red-rumped swallows. Most of all, I felt grateful to Su, for giving me a whole night of his affections. After this, I knew my timidity would subside, and I would go about as fearlessly as I had before the murder.

I knocked my glass against Su's.

"Su, long life to your mother! Good luck and happiness to you and Swallow!"

2009

››› **Editor's Notes:**

1. Huamatou appears elsewhere in the issue as "Flowery Pier Town".

Critique

The Enlightened Way of Fiction

— A close reading of two short stories by Ye Mi

Zhang Xuexin / 张学昕
Translated by Ella Schwalb

Zhang Xuexin / 张学昕

I

In 1997, when she was thirty-three, Ye Mi published a novella called "Metamorphosis." Right from the get-go, she displayed an awareness of fiction that was different than her peers, a different orientation of the spirit and a different aesthetic bearing. She was born in the mid-1960s, but in both form and approach, her writing is nothing like the 60s writers, or the so-called 70s style. Even from the perspective of "gender," there is an outstanding singularity in both the appearance and structure of her fiction: in her natural and unrestrained narrative style, she integrates into an organic hybrid the meticulous gentleness of female writers with the broad vigor of their male counterparts. Remarkably, her writing has only gotten increasingly solid and generous over the course of the subsequent twenty years. Her understanding of the art of fiction, her feeling for it and her expressive power, have made her one of the most important fiction writers of the contemporary era, and one who has maintained her own particular high standard of writing throughout.

Ye Mi's first batch of novellas were almost all related to "growth." Growth is a painful metamorphosis, and Ye Mi did her utmost in presenting this difficult and complicated process, taking it as an angle and mode through which she understands life and the world. I get the sense that in her series of so-called "Bildungsroman" Ye Mi is, without a doubt, also speaking to life and times in the complex context of 20th century Chinese society—people's destinies, psyches and the wavering journeys of their souls. She comprehended and examined an innovative core value system by contemplating the tangle of her characters' fates—of their dislocations and disturbances—in the historical circumstances of these extraordinary times, and we can get a precise sense of the veracity of these stories and characters. In their transformations and evolutions, people's psyches and souls have boundless appeal and vitality when rendered by Ye Mi's pen. She persistently chooses these subjects for her writing, and there is an unmistakable depth in her unique style.

Ye Mi seems to possess an innate gift for writing fiction. There are no marks of an amateur in any of the stories from her early period, such as "Metamorphosis," "The Holy Light of Jesus," "Two Lifetimes of Sorrow," and "Pink Night." It looks almost as though, in her own writing, she never goes through any sort of acute process of transformation from development to maturity. She keeps her distance from all sorts of trends in the 80s and 90s, going her own way with the muted style and spirit of her writing, and the natural simplicity of her narratives. Placing her only within the bounds of feminist discourse would clearly be crude and careless; likewise, it would be a restrictively narrow definition to sum up the bulk of Ye Mi's fiction simply as "Bildungsroman." Fiction that is hard to classify is, I think, the mark of a mature writer. In terms of narrative aesthetics, there seems to be an elegance, and a hint of classicism in her work, simple and humble without relying too much on technique, yet still nimbly transmitting beauty amid the vicissitudes of the earthly world. Her narratives suggest a streak of influences from bygone styles, and to this day I have yet to truly make sense of it. I have thought for quite some time that her works must contain some kind of secret "profound theory." But she would never rashly lay it bare between the lines of her stories, because Ye Mi does not condescend to those kinds of peculiar, vapid sentiments in the slightest. In her simple elegance, she always harbors lofty expectations for her own heart.

There is a plain quality that has always defined the essential features of Ye Mi as a person, and of her writing. It may be that it is precisely the pursuit and maintenance of this quality—be it conscious or unconscious—that has made her even more adept in the domain of everyday life, clearing away both vulgarity and pain. With a pious heart and a reverential intent, her tranquil writing is as lucid and smooth as silk, and leaves a rich aftertaste.

In fact, Ye Mi's writing continually maintains this easy-going approach, and always preserves her "original intent," which I think is mainly rooted in her "enlightened heart." My first encounter with Ye Mi's "enlightened heart" was actually not through her writing at all, but rather through spending time with her a few years ago. There is one small episode in particular that I will never forget.

In early April of 2013, the two magazines *Commentary on Contemporary Writers* and *Writers* hosted "The Elite Forum on Contemporary Chinese Short

Fiction" in Yixing. Several contemporary experts and critics of fiction took part in the conference, including Su Tong (苏童), Liu Qingbang (刘庆邦), Ge Fei (格非), Fan Xiaoqing (范小青), Zong Renfa (宗仁发), Zhang Xinying (张新颖), Wang Shou (王手), and of course, Ye Mi. She came on time for check-in on the first day, but the conference had a little bit of an unusual schedule—the first thing planned for the second day was a visit of the surrounding locale. Speeches and discussions on the conference topic weren't set to start until the third day. But Ye Mi skipped the visit on the second day, and instead rushed to drive back home to Suzhou, saying she would be sure to hurry back to Yixing in time for the meetings on day three. Why did she go out of her way to shuttle back and forth like that? It was actually for a stray cat she had just adopted. The cat was missing some teeth and had trouble eating, so it needed to be fed manually. Many people were puzzled—is it really worth it to drive 400 kilometers round trip for a disabled stray cat? I heard later that she took in a great number of lost or abandoned stray cats and dogs, and that, along with the few chickens, ducks, geese and dogs she had in her yard, they formed one big animal family. That's when I decided to take another look at Ye Mi as a writer. What kind of structure and presence would such a kindhearted writer use in her work? What kind of angle and attitude would she take in her examinations of humanity and of this complicated, fickle world? My expectations for Ye Mi grew even greater; through this other side of her, I had learned about the softness of her heart——her "enlightened heart."

II

Ye Mi's fiction actually demonstrates quite a lot of "Discipline to the Way." This "Way" is both the Way of humanism and the Way of the Buddha. It is also the Path of fiction. To put it simply, this Way is the driving force of the innermost spirit or soul of Ye Mi's writing—the enlightened

Way of fiction. Naturally, it is rooted in her enlightened heart, which is also precisely what enables her fiction to constantly transform the inertia of previous narrative orientations in such extraordinary ways, thereby making progress according to the feelings and ideas of "enlightenment."

There is no fixed method for writing fiction, and it is extremely difficult to find some kind of soul that can be sustained by a short story. What is the reason for writing a short story? And what does it mean, for a writer and her text, to write a character's fate and mode of existence? In other words, how should a short story's capacity ultimately be understood? Short stories have their own structure, while novels have their own scope. But regardless of structure or scope, the meaning of a text depends on the capacity of its value. So, how much value will Ye Mi's enlightened Way of fiction add to the genre of the short story?

Of course, fiction has no set laws; every writer has their own familiar or favored routines, and every piece of writing, too, works according to its own logic and has its own unique essence. What is the primary force behind a piece of fiction? And what keeps it going? There are enormous differences between all writers and all texts, and in fact, a writer's moral conduct depends on her own way of being, expressing her way of looking at others, her way of handling the relationships between people, the world, and everything in it. In a way, it is also a form of looking for proof of life and of matter. According to Jia Pingwa's (贾平凹) formulation, "A material object is taken as existent, objective matter, and the essence of its existence is meaningful according to its utility. But when writing treats the entirety as an image, it needs to use concrete matter—that is, the routines of life—to be complete. Life has patterns for its own flow; it keeps going day after day. Smooth or rocky—it all must pass. Such is life itself, in its chaos and its vitality. So, the more concretely something is written, the more it comes to life; and the more abstractly it is written, the more imagery there is." [1] So I think Ye Mi's fiction also finds the "utility" of material objects and existence, and when showing the course of life and its concrete matter, she relies on her own writerly judgment in presenting their patterns and utility. Perhaps, this is what constitutes the enlightened Way of life. Only once a writer clearly sorts out the "enlightened Way" in life can she take life and matter and enter into the enlightened Way of fiction.

Honestly, each and every one of Ye Mi's texts could hold up against a close reading, but I think those pieces that touch upon Buddhism, the Way, and Zen are among her most unforgettable. Of the various genres in which she writes, my favorites, naturally, are her short stories. And of her short stories, my favorites are "Bright Moon Temple" and the recently-published "Snowflake Meditation." What's more, I get the feeling in some of the other stories I've read, such as "An Eagle Fading Away at Potala" and "Rising Alone," that her fiction is constantly exploring the "spirit zone" between "withdrawing from the world" and "participating in the world" —whether intentionally or otherwise. She is always trying to capture the ephemeral and the transcendental potential from within the immensity of the earthly world. In fact, this transcendence takes place when a writer transcends herself through her work. Early on, Ye Mi said the following about her goals and intentions for writing, "I confess that my motivation for writing is this simple: I couldn't live without it. My writing has maintained this can't-live-without-it feeling, which I am unwilling to abandon, because when I'm feeling good, it gives me a sudden feeling of calmness, and it doesn't let me get proud for very long. I'm always watching my step, staying away from any murky waters. It also clears away my desires for fame and fortune; it keeps me from wanting it all." [2] She vows to write because she can't live without it, and filters out her desires for fame and fortune—these are the kinds of feelings and convictions from which she writes. Rooted in her stories are the dualities of rationality and emotion, fact and fiction, flashiness and moderation. They are all well controlled, and they all stand out from the ordinary.

The short story "Bright Moon Temple" was written in 2003. I remember that the first thing that occurred to me when I finished reading it was a short story by Mr. Wang Zengqi (汪曾祺) called "Taking Oaths," published in the 1980s. The old couple Master Luo and Master Bo, who are in charge of Bright Moon Temple in Ye Mi's story, immediately called to mind Mingzi and Little Yingzi in "Taking Oaths." The difference is that the boy-girl duo in "Taking Oaths" is much younger. But these two generations of stories, "Taking Oaths" and "Bright Moon Temple," convey different qualities according to their writers' ages and experiences: the former's tone is bright, while the latter's is largely gloomy and depressed. The former shows the beauty of humanity in a symbiosis of vitality and simplicity, giving it an air of plenty, while the latter shows a complicated tangle of fates, giving it a subdued, grave feeling. The former is clear, while the latter is fuzzy and ambiguous. Scholar Sun Yu (孙郁) praised "Taking Oaths," by saying, "In its limpid and pure childish innocence, there is a feeling of earthly things falling away, and the spirit coming closer. The beauty of the human world and the charm of life are quietly, leisurely highlighted. In the course of a hundred years, only a scant few people can produce this kind of style." [3] There is nothing lukewarm about Sun Yu's assessment, which enthusiastically endorses Wang Zengqi's work. And while the narrative in "Bright Moon Temple," written by a woman, doesn't have the same ruthless efficiency as the former, the story is told skillfully, with expertise. The setting is natural and pleasant, and the characters are neither over-described nor under-described, everything done with an unhurried ease that doesn't fail to impress. Her story poignantly tells of the harshness of life and the fickleness of social trends, showing how Zen can also be found in the ways of the earthly world. It is clear that both write about the beauty of the earthly world within the domain of Buddhist traditions, but they diverge in that "Bright Moon Temple" is permeated by a dim, latent pain and a faint sorrow and suffering, which together wrap this ordinary couple and their temple life within a crisp, cool layer of poetic sentiment. I'm still making conjectures, trying to figure it all out—could it be that the old couple are Mingzi and Little Yingzi in the future? Or could it be that they are reincarnations of one another in a different lifetime? Perhaps that is why I instinctively drew a connection between the two stories.

In fact, both the narrative and structure of "Bright Moon Temple" are brimming with tremendous suspense, with the complications of life and the world, and the imagined and implicit mysteries of space-time. The narrative is also full of blank space and tension. Why did this ordinary, secular couple choose this run-of-the-mill little temple to live in for thirty years in the first place? Why does the female protagonist's "joyful look only just barely [brush] across her face before quickly being replaced by a faint dolefulness?" In their indifferent peacefulness and their simple sincerity, they have a boundless adoration for secular, commonplace, ordinary life—so why did they make a home of this little temple, letting a few decades pass by as though it were no more than a single day, living out the rest of their lives in this tranquility? What secret past has this couple lived through? What kinds of major misfortunes impacted their life, those thirty years ago? They are unusual, mysterious "monks," who never talk about their past with anyone. How much hidden anguish must they hold in their innermost beings that they would choose to spend their whole lives in a temple? When all is said and done, is theirs a life of release, or a life of abandonment? On the surface, their relationship with Buddhism seems neither too close nor too distant: fate and karma seem to be immensely profound secrets that are hidden in the text, and dormant in their hearts. The mental distance between the narrator and the couple collapse after just a fleeting interaction, which, simple and honest as it is, serves as a bridge between them. Yet the narrator's persistent inquiries are almost enough to brutally push the couple's psyches and spirits into the abyss of pain.

> *The line came back to me: "What kinds of things count as wrongs?"*
>
> *The question had sunk the room into a sudden spell of silence. The silence arose abruptly, but it made sense, I thought. We all felt that we'd been brought together by fate, and there was too much we wanted to say to each other. We fell into a strange position: in that brief moment that had just flitted by, we all longed for one another.*
>
> *But we just stared at each other, and nobody said a word. Bygone dreams swept by like precious fleeting glances.*
>
> ...
>
> *I turned to them and said, "Master Bo, people say you two came here in the spring of 1970. It's been thirty years, and no one has ever come to visit you."*
>
> *Master Bo immediately looked to Master Luo, who quickly pulled her into their room, and bolted up the door in a flurry. All this happened in the space of one distracted blink, and by the time I realized what was happening, the door was already closed. I stood in the hallway completely dull, and feeling a twinge of guilt.*
>
> *I had been sleeping fitfully for who knows how long, when I was awakened by a sound. I opened my eyes and saw the sleek moonlight outside, shining as bright as day. The wind had stopped, and all the trees and clusters of flowers stood upright and still. Full of dread, I perked up my ears and listened closely to find out where the sound was coming from. I heard a*

weeping sound, as delicate as silk ... that's right, it was the sound of weeping, coming from Master Bo and Master Luo's room.

This inevitably raises some questions, and perhaps it is just like Ye Mi wrote in the story: "Making conjectures is a gloomy business." Initially inspired by a simple desire to enter the world of flowers and plants, this young woman who adores life, who thirsts for it and is determined to seek it out, inadvertently treads into the realm of a secret existence. Luo and Bo, the married couple, are mutually dependent, and linger between the bounds of Buddhism and the secular world, seeming to drift through life by laying low. They live in the enlightened Way—neither set free nor attached. Yet they never stray too far from the secular world: they still have worries and human feelings, and are well aware of worldly fluctuations. They marvel at life, have respect for the soul, and live in a way that is neither too arrogant nor too humble. Maybe they are simply able to use their gentle mentality to break free from the hopelessness of days gone by, which may ultimately be the best choice for entering into a world of freedom. But, I don't think that Ye Mi leaves the suspense fully unresolved. When the narrator revisits Bright Moon Temple a few months later, she sadly learns that Master Bo has died from sickness, and that Master Luo has left to a different temple to officially become a monk, and the riddles of the couple's past are left untold. But Ye Mi doesn't see their history as important at all, and the many questions of the past vanish like clouds of smoke, obscured by the present reality. Through the text, she tries to show how the protagonists bear the weight of their destiny, waiting with stoicism and composure.

I think that in the grand scheme of human nature and feelings, as long as one can still perceive the existence of beauty, it is possible to achieve a state of grief without blame, of injury without anger—regardless of what kinds of misfortune one may have endured in the past. Life will continue to have its wonderful sparks, and by salvaging scraps of ordinary life and history, Ye Mi strives to reconcile the fragmentariness and wholeness of humble folks' souls, and to reconstruct the true conditions of their existence.

The most important aspect of this short story is, I think, how it leaves empty space in the narrations of histories, both of regular people's individual existences and fate, and in the major historical events of a society. This is actually a literary technique to handle complicated matters with seeming lightness. When her characters were young, they came up against some adversity or discord in the social instability of that era—did it really take thirty years' time to mend or be redeemed? Can the heaviness of life, or of history in particular, really be reduced to a bearable lightness within thirty years? How are major historical events deeply implicated in an individual's inner life, and how does an individual's innermost being, in turn, constitute the depths of history? What happened back then, after all? Something must not have happened, right? Will later generations make light of it? Ye Mi seems to be writing a dream—or rather the nightmare of two ordinary people. Yet she never writes what actually happened in the dream itself, starting instead from the "conclusion." She develops that enormous hidden anguish of personal existence, catching her characters in a moment or two of their many long years. Although they situated themselves within a Buddhist temple, their souls could not find peace, nor could they easily cast off the sediments of history and the tangles and vexations at the core of the earthly world. In a sense, they were living elsewhere the whole time.

The story's structure is not circular, rather it resembles an oval plaza with many roads radiating off from it, stretching in all directions. This structure is also suggestive of the way the characters do not know which course to follow when choosing their destinies. The narrative maintains a balance of moderate dimensions throughout, suggesting the closely guarded secrets of major historical events through the conditions of the daily existence of the lowest rungs of society, reflecting human vitality, and fully affirming humanity's tenacity, warmth and kindheartedness. Never does it crudely adopt a contemptuous attitude or deal frivolously with the complicated relationships between people's spirits and their living environments. Within the flow of details and particulars, we comprehend the vast and hazy expansiveness of history and the affairs of human life. But, perhaps owing to the limitations of the story's perspective, the over-simplification of the characters' relationships confines the text's imaginative space, which inevitably influences and limits the story's otherwise greater tension. But perhaps this is just an impossible paradox of the short story genre.

III

In my opinion, "Snowflake Meditation" is one of the best Ye Mi short stories I have read to date. It can also be considered as a representative work of her narratives with thick overtones of the "enlightened Way" and "moral conduct."

We will first of all confront the basic question of what can or should be done when a "dandy" who enjoyed a lifetime of freedom, merriment and fancy, finds himself enveloped by the war panic, with alarms ringing on all sides as the enemy soldiers approach the city walls, ready to siege. He Wenjian, a local big shot, opts to flee. Perhaps we can take it one step further to really get to the heart of the matter: Why, after all, did Ye Mi write about this man of leisure who prizes "life" above all else, even in the midst of imminent war? These questions are precisely why I am so keenly looking forward to analyzing this character and parsing this story.

Is writing a character who can't be defined by any single ideology a good starting point for a story's success? He Wenjian has, to a large degree, a classical air to him; he is a man of earthly pleasures with the heart of a literati. How should the existence of a "good person" be described and judged in the particular context of war?

There's no doubt that He Wenjian has his own stubborn philosophy—in fact, there's no need to debate the matter. For He Wenjian, there is no phrase more suitable than "personality is fate." In his instinctive decision to escape, he seems to have already broken from the virtues of patriotism. Writing the moment-to-moment reality of a person's daily life in the context of war is actually quite a difficult task. Is there anyone capable of maintaining a sense of normalcy in his life when the flames of war are raging? What counts as maintaining one's integrity? Actually, according to traditional Chinese personality criteria, He Wenjian is adequately equipped in terms of moral strength; it is just that he is a little unwise when it comes to good judgment. So what view should we take of him, when it comes right down to it?

The world described in this story is ice-cold and jittery—everyone is panicking, and treating one another like enemies. Yet, a few fine gleams of warmth still make their force felt, in spite of the frozen desolation of these chaotic times. This is what gives the story its warmth. Ye Mi clearly takes a warm, lenient view towards human nature in her understanding and forgiveness, and in her striving to reach the Buddhist state of mind. As such, the narrative is able to present the conditions of existence in all their veracity and possibilities. In normal circumstances, He Wenjian's moral character could be summarized and described as such: he doesn't want his lot to be extremely tragic or miserable. He is unwilling to despair, and even less willing to stand in the eye of the storm, preferring to be flexible and adaptable, going with the flow instead of resisting the forces of nature. There's nothing blameworthy about this at all. This kind and charitable scholar who so ardently loves freedom and romantic themes was entirely incapable of adapting to and accepting the reality of all the great changes brought about by war. His former life was coming to a close, and he had a few options: he could avoid the war in order to survive, he could get angry, he could cry, he could flee, or he could keep cool under fire and respond calmly. But he was reluctant to be torn from his former life. Numbing oneself can be deemed a form of happiness, even if it is only a meager happiness found in adversity. It seems as though he never dared to reflect psychologically too deeply, since reflection would immediately give rise to suffering. Over a very short stretch of time he strove to constantly pull his own mental state back to self-awareness, into an illusion, seeking to make peace with his fate in his practice of Zen. "He couldn't help but think that in the long rivers of history, he was no more than a purposeless nobody who wouldn't hurt a fly. How could anyone make such a big fuss over taking his life?" So, before his escape from the coming war, he went to Murmur Temple and meditated on the snowy ground, "sitting in oblivion" with a "heart of abstinence." It's clear that the pursuits he forged for his free and cheerful temperament, cultivated ever since he was young, have been utterly unalterable throughout his whole life.

Murmur Temple let him find a bit of breathing room and tranquility in a hollow moral code. When thoughts are held captive, some people choose compliance, while others choose resistance, and still others choose betrayal, modifying their values to meet changing life demands. To He Wenjian, it is very clear that going against the grain would be difficult, and may even be deadly. "Non-doing," becomes his adaptive philosophy. Non-doing allows for self-defense, self-respect, and self-confidence—it's a form of self-maintenance, a form of patient and necessary endurance that also contains an element of justice, and which may, in the end, be considered a sort of logic for social conduct, a mode of life. This is He Wenjian's rare wisdom. After all, this tale is ultimately showing a way of life. The most profound truth is also the simplest, and the principles of He Wenjian's attitude even have a bit of humor to them, as he is adept at playing down the agony and severity of reality to find a momentary joy, which is at the same time accompanied by a calm and sober generosity of benign neglect. In the past, his method for maintaining his own mental balance served him well for living a free and easy life. The core of his temperament is his compassion; he has selfish desires, loves life ardently, cares for people, and doesn't want there to be volatile, disastrous crises. He is also unwilling to turn the other cheek, or to be reduced to a traitor: it's only natural—a very common occurrence. People are just passing travelers who cannot decide their own destinies. He Wenjian wants only to return to his innermost being, so he meditates in search of the Way, so completely absorbed that he doesn't want to come back out of it. People are just social animals, and it's hard to make simplistic distinctions between the good and the bad. As Ye Mi writes it, He Wenjian leads a very complicated existence. It is only after dispelling any intimations of the divine or the ideological that the narrative achieves such effortlessness, and the writing shares its soft, lingering flavor.

Chewing over He Wenjian's options really leaves us with a strong sense of ambivalence. But when it comes down to it, he is a nobody in the grand scheme of things. But while he may not be able to write history, he can retain his personal integrity without letting go of the roots of his own soul. I think, at the very least he should be able to avert dishonor, if not death. We cannot demand that he go to battle when he doesn't even have the strength to truss a chicken. Neither a drifter nor a turncoat, he chose to escape. We could call it a philosophy of adaptation and survival, or we could just say that, while the world was in chaos, he sought to maintain his personal integrity without intending to seek fame and influence—but in either case we can see that these are the moves someone makes when their life is in jeopardy and they are left without options. Or are we too alienated nowadays to understand people in this way? At the end of the day, should we understand him and sympathize with him? Or should we be like his student Pan Xinbei, and compel him at all costs to go to battle? Pan Xinbei may never understand that his teacher actually has a powerful sense of selfhood.

In fact, these days it is incredibly difficult for us to re-describe an era that has already faded away. History gets ever more vague in the complicated mess of competing value systems and the din of competing voices. So, what's the purpose of recreating the life of this little nobody? Is it ultimately a matter of reviving the history of an ordinary person's individual life, or is it a matter of re-exploring and reviewing the conditions of the soul of a past era, in order to examine the meaning and values of our current existence? It goes without saying that Ye Mi's text leaves us a lot of interpretive space.

But we aren't in it alone. Ye Mi appears to be using an awareness of the enlightened Way or Zen to interpret He Wenjian's attitude towards life and his choices. In the text, she appraises her characters with value-neutral judgments—because people cannot be reduced to a simple binary of sublime or pathetic; they are so much more than that. It's clear that Ye Mi controlled her feelings when writing this character and this story. She restrained herself to the greatest extent possible so as not to let her emotions overflow. She used a non-moralizing writing style that is permeated throughout with a humanizing aesthetic, in search of those things that are most true and most distinctive about the earthly world. It encompasses brightness and gloom, suggesting both good and evil, both beauty and ugliness, all of which unfold lightly and calmly on the level that transcends the secular world. In the space of Ye Mi's understanding, He Wenjian's "Zen" is a "Snowflake Meditation." It is the location or manner of his "mental concentration," his "non-persistence" ; it is the pull and prompting of the Buddha, the Way, Zen, and the mind. It is a kind of "tranquil contemplation," which can only be carried out in a certain frame of mind, in his favorite haunt. In other words,

He Wenjian is struggling on the threshold between the earthly world and "adherence," yet he is frequently incapable of controlling himself. This is because he always wants to live according to his own mode of life. The relationship between an individual's choices and the era in which he lives is inevitably paradoxical; the two are always intertwined. It's clear that when reading Ye Mi's stories, we will invariably end up thinking of a great many things beyond the scope of the text itself.

We may also be wondering about what forces control and determine the narrative of a short story and its capacity, as well as in what ways the flavor, tone, feeling and atmosphere buried in the story can grow over-complicated, like a thicket with too many branches. As the characters dictate the course and cadence of the narrative, pain and worldliness are all transformed and made visible through her writing, slowly flowing out to the readers. This effect cannot be achieved simply through technical tricks, but must undoubtedly demonstrate a profound understanding of the short story genre, and furthermore a deep love of living and respect for all life.

So I understand why Ye Mi's fiction never indulges in tasteless histrionics. I believe that for her, writing must be a joyful, rigorous, and sublime occupation. "Being like the movement of the skies in constant self-improvement, and also infinitely generous and tolerant like the earth." Perhaps it is exactly this mentality—this willingness to accept other people's views, and this ardent love of writing—that makes Ye Mi who she is.

I've heard that Ye Mi lives on Lake Tai in the outskirts of Suzhou, where she has a rustic countryside "estate" , with a dizzying variety of all sorts of flowers, plants, and trees, fruits and vegetables, and chickens, ducks, geese, dogs and cats. Ye Mi is in contact with these things every day as she toils away cheerfully, routinely learning from all kinds of past and present experiences. She comprehends life in the earthly world, the human world and all living things, with lyricism and with gravity, with poetry and with wisdom, writing in a smartly refined, understated way that always hits home, and frequently looks back upon the dust of history. Moreover, she is always able to find new narrative perspectives and expressions for her demands for herself. In her narratives, she seeks both the commonplace and the transcendent, the complexity within the ordinary, and the melancholy contained in leisure, seeking an elegant beauty in simplicity, always savoring of the earthly world. In the end, she unfolds an expansive freedom, both in her writing and in her life.

I think these are the states of being she longs to reach, and which she is surely capable of reaching.

››› **Notes:**

1. Jia Pingwa: *On Fiction*, page 115, SDX Joint Publishing Company, 2015 Issue.
2. Ye Mi: "A Dream of Being Able to Walk" , in "Jiangsu Writers Study—Ye Mi Chapter" , page 21, Fudan University Press 2009 Issue.
3. Sun Yu: "Scholar-Official of the Revolutionary Era: Memoirs of Wang Zengqi" , page 164, SDX Joint Publishing Company, 2014 Issue.

Interview

An Interview with Ye Mi

Jin Ying / 金　莹
Translated by Shelly Bryant

Jin Ying: Anyone who eventually engages in literary writing almost certainly harbored literary aspirations in his/her childhood, and many who are active in literary writing today gained fame when they were young. But judging from your experience, you seem to be a late-comer. I read in an article that your first piece of published work was *A Renowned Cook*, which was based on a relative who served as a cook for a top government official. This was followed by your most widely acclaimed work, *Metamorphosis*. What did you do before you started writing? What prompted you to start your literary career? What were the circumstances that drove you in this direction?

Ye Mi: When I was six, I went with my parents to "settle down in the countryside", a political movement of that time. There I learnt to fight and quarrel, as well as to read. Though I did not read much as an adult, I read many books when I was a teenager, including classic and modern writing in Chinese, along with numerous works translated from French, German and Russian. Some of these books were owned by my family, while some were borrowed. Some I came by easily and read with a light mood, while others were hard-earned and read with a heavy heart. When I was in the third year of primary school, I was sent from the countryside of northern Jiangsu Province to stay with one of my relatives in Suzhou, hoping to continue with my fourth year of schooling. The relative asked me to babysit their child. Once while babysitting, I was reading a revolutionary book with a blue labour-union library seal on its cover about female militia on islands, a book I had borrowed from a female neighbor. I was scolded for that, and the book was torn to pieces. When I went to tell the neighbor, I didn't have a book to return to her, so I stood outside her door, not knowing what to say. She grabbed a handful of popcorn that her daughter who was roughly my age, with pretty, wavy hair was eating, put in my hands, and said not to worry about the book. She went on to scold her daughter for not reading, taking me as a role model who stuck at reading even in plight.

I don't know why I loved reading so much when I was small, but I do remember this respectable neighbour who helped me to see for the first time in my life that reading was a good thing. I had quite an unsettled life. It was not until my own child started primary school that I settled down with a small house I had built myself, no longer having to move around frequently. I had a stable job too, working in the same district governmental compound as my husband. I was merely an accountant, but it seemed that to a large degree, I had my own way of thinking as a result of my early reading. I later quit my job because I was at odds with my boss.

It was when I got back home after quitting my job that I began to think about my life. Fortunately, my father owned a small company, where I went to work as an accountant. Since there were two other responsible accountants and I didn't need to do the bookkeeping or the management, I had more than enough time to myself, so I started to write. I started with *A Renowned Cook*, and moved on to another two short stories, published in *Yuhua*. I then moved onto the novella, *Metamorphosis*.

A Renowned Cook was published in *Suzhou Journal.* I based it on one of my relatives, who had worked as Lin Biao's cook and was known as the "King of Cooking in the Yangtze River region." I stayed at his home for a while when I was a toddler. His wife looked after me, saying that I was notorious for crying very loud, especially late at night when everyone in the village was asleep and my noisy crying was the only sound to be heard. I believe what she said was true, and I guess I was just an unloved child craving love since I was very small. This might be my motive for writing.

Jin Ying: The first of your works that I read was *Metamorphosis*, and I felt I could identify with the younger brother, who wavered between his ideals and reality, sometimes easily giving in, while other times sticking to what he believes, and always doubting what he once believed and feeling he would never get through his prolonged adolescence. It's safe to say that the novella has touched and impacted many growing youths, as it has greatly impacted me. You have mentioned in some of your articles that the younger brother is, in a sense, part of you. Looking back on the work that established your prestige, how would you evaluate it now?

Ye Mi: *Metamorphosis* is set against the backdrop of China's reform and opening-up. Honestly speaking, I have been negative about this sweeping nationwide economic surge, as I feel that we Chinese are not yet ready for the transition, the fundamental reason being that we have not gone through a thorough thought process. Not being ready, my "younger brother" was lost, agonized, and compromised, which is a picture of everyone's spiritual journey, including my own. We have suffered for seeking truth, we were lost when struggling for survival, and in the end, we are back on the track of moderation, becoming individuals with clear minds and compromising actions, even giving in beyond what is necessary. It might be justifiable to make compromises on big things, but why do we do so with small things as well? What is it we are afraid of? It is ourselves. We are not focused enough, and our mind stops working when we are stuck. Even when it doesn't, it goes on a different path, eventually becoming uncontrollable. This is why my "younger brother" will never grow up.

A couple of years ago, I thought of writing a sequel to *Metamorphosis*. I even had the story in mind, but I ended up not writing it. My "younger brother" will not have any other ending, except further decline. This is also what we have seen in recent years.

Looking back on *Metamorphosis*, I am still filled with agony. Although it is about a particular incident in a particular time, sadly we have made zero progress in the sixteen or seventeen years since. True, we're still learning—from

WeChat. I hope one day when I look back on *Metamorphosis*, I'll not feel agonized but pleased, just the way we feel about China when we see North Korea today.

Jin Ying: In *A Sketch Book of Romance*, Kong Yanni is a girl in her adolescence. In your first novel *Beautiful Youth*, Li Bu'an is a boy in his teenage years. It seems that you are quite fond of writing about girls and boys at this age. Is this because you went from the countryside back to the city at this age? The change in places undoubtedly impacts a sensitive girl. How was your life in the countryside? And how did that period in your life influence your writing?

Ye Mi: I went to the countryside at the age of six because my whole family was "reduced" to living there. According to the policy, one family member could stay in town, so my parents kept my *hukou*, or registered domicile, in Suzhou, where I went at ten, hoping to continue with my schooling. But this was all in vain, and I had to go back to the countryside in northern Jiangsu. At 14, when I finished my second year study in secondary school, I went back to Suzhou alone. As a result, for most of my teenage years, I felt quite lonely and detached from the city, which was not particularly congenial to a young person like me. What I saw was frightening demonstrations and fights between husbands and wives or wives and parents-in-law. The fights between kids were different from those in the countryside, where things were settled in simple ways: by fighting or cursing. I had always seen myself as a kid from the countryside, and my peers in town saw me that way, too, but I was not exactly a rural kid. The failure to identify myself accurately brought me great confusion and an inner conflict as big as the gap between the urban and rural areas.

Before I went to primary school, I was sent to stay with four different families in Shanghai, Suzhou, and Wuxi. Apart from the "King of Cooking in the Yangtze River region" , the other three families were all city people who struck me as weird, or at times even frightening. They were workers, craftsmen, and members of the intelligentsia, but in the eyes of a young person, they were unhappy, disadvantaged, and violent, people who would vent their frustrations on me, hitting me and frequently slapping me. But in front of outsiders, they behaved extremely humbly.

Country life looks simple, but it is not exactly so. During that oppressive historical period, abnormalities occurred in numbed people's lives. I saw first-hand that sad farmers had to cut down their pear trees in their own fields, that good neighbours would fight fiercely for a seedling, that an unmarried woman had to give birth to a baby in the open, that a quiet old teacher cut his wrist to commit suicide, and that a middle-aged female headmaster threw her baby in a cesspool after its birth. Meanwhile, I also saw the most concentrated groups of fireflies, the most luxuriant wild grasslands, and the most bleak cemeteries. Along with the books I have read, these offered me boundless space for my imagination, blurring reality and fantasy, dream and imagination.

Jin: *A Sketch Book of Romance* involves what happened during the Cultural Revolution, which is a heated and sensitive topic taken up in many novels in recent years. The word "romance" tends to be misinterpreted. It can refer to those people who are talented in letters and live unconventional lifestyles, or to one's romantic entanglements. What prompted you to write this novel? What was on your mind when you tied "romance" to that unique period of time?

The novel also touches upon people's craving for and practice of sex, which connects the intelligentsia with activists, revolutionaries with landowners, and revolutionaries with themselves. Such depictions are not made out of curiosity or an attempt to choke what ought to be said. Instead, they are more of the daily, normal routine, subtle and natural. These days, descriptions of sex are either over- or underdone, but depictions in this novel will definitely disappoint those who are simply curious and slightly embarrass those who act as moral guards. What is most controversial about the novel is the descriptions of teenage girls' craving for sex. Did you think about that when writing? Is it part of your intention to highlight average people's longing for humanity, which even revolution will not stifle?

Ye Mi: You're right; love and sex are the themes of the novel. Six years ago when I planned to write the novel, I did some interviews, from which I saw that Chinese people have never ceased to pursue love, despite various hardships. I was deeply impressed and touched. Even during a fanatical period of revolution, people engaged in a constant pursuit of beauty, love, and sex, suggesting individual identity and everlasting humanity.

As for possible controversies, I didn't think much about that, except to note that I, as a female writer, needed to be mentally prepared to write about sex. After all, it's often unpleasant for the reader when a woman writes about sex. But what I intended to write was the sexual life in love or family relations, physical or metaphysical, which is natural and beautiful as long as it remains human.

We also know that China has undergone a time when human nature was suppressed, and cities and rural areas decayed. But when the right time comes, people will always resume their persistent, admirable pursuit of love, which is what we stay alive for. Actually the story is not yet complete. It is half of my novel, and the other half is not yet complete. It is set approximately between 1978 and 1988. Ye Kai and Cheng Yongxin, respectively my editor and the editor-in-chief of *Harvest*, suggested publishing the first half on their journal because, having read my manuscript, they felt the two parts could be separately published, as they both stand alone. I followed their advice, and when the other half is done, I'll take it as a continuation of *A Sketch Book of Romance*, making it a series.

The word "*romance*" has two connotations: the characters' spirit and their lives. The idea I have intended to express is, quoting Chairman Mao, "In seeking talented and romantic people, we need to look to today's society." There are many other talented, romantic individuals who strive to pursue excellence. It's just that we don't know them well enough yet.

JinYing: In *A Sketch Book of Romance*, traditional villains and victims seem to be somewhat different from the typical depictions of such figures in literary works. Wang Enlai is a villain, but you didn't concentrate on his tremendous inner change or his father's defense of him. You wrote about the pride of the intelligentsia, peace in a crazy, conflicting time, and the pursuit of love, the romantic life for which you were stingy with words. You also presented their vulnerability, such as Grandpa Liu's gullibility to land himself into the labor camp and the father's overnight ageing, which were both unexpected but natural, as revolutionists have their soft spots and repentance as well. Does this perspective (i.e., not an emotional accusation, but a more multi-dimensional presentation, with an open ending and no judgment: with bad and good people carrying on with their lives) have something to do with your personal perception of the Cultural Revolution? How did the revolution you experienced for a short while impact your life as one born in 1964?

Ye Mi: In the second half of the novel, from 1978 to 1988, I wrote about the "fate" unique to both good and bad people. When life is more unstable and society more irrational, humanity is confronted with unprecedented challenges.

Jin Ying: I personally feel that the writing techniques in this novel are quite complicated. When I'm reading, I sense the skill and flavor of conventional novels. Many transitory characters and episodes in your novels can be treated as fascinating short stories capable of standing on their own, for instance, Du Ke and his partner stopping cars for the road-check as an experiment. In terms of writing skills, what were your considerations at the beginning of the writing process? From what has been said, you conceived this story on the bus from the countryside to the city.

Short stories and novels vary greatly in length and structure. How do you handle these differences while writing?

Ye Mi: Novels embrace ideas, while short stories embrace inspiration. The latter present things quite differently from the former. They are light, to the point, and surprising. Further, the narration in short stories serves for inspiration, while in novels, it is about ideas. It's true that from time to time, ideas need inspiration as the pioneer, while inspiration relies on ideas as a guise. But the fundamental difference is that inspiration is like a single stream going into the sea, while ideas are numerous rivers flowing into the sea. The former matures when taking shape, instantaneously, like a child who learns to walk the moment he/she touches the ground. By comparison, ideas need time to take shape, grow up, and mature, like the peaches in the orchard of the Queen of Heaven, which take 3,000 years to blossom, another 3,000 years to bear fruit, and still another 3,000 years to mature.

When writing this novel, I knew what I intended to express, but I was not fully prepared, so I started to conceive of the characters on the hours-long bus trips between the rural and urban areas. By the time I began to write, I was still taking notes, reading loads of books, and conducting many interviews. This trivial work is beneficial to writers, just as one end of a kite remains on the ground no matter how high it flies, lest it go out of control.

When writing novels, the issue is whether you have much to talk about, not the framework or inspiration.

Jin Ying: In many of your stories, the characters seem to have dreams that are at odds with reality. For instance, the velvet as tender as sister Yao's skin in "Velvet" , the pretty woman far away in Qingdao in *Beautiful Youth*, or Tibet in *Metamorphosis*. These otherwise ordinary things in the mundane world should turn into something unattainable. What do you have to consider when focusing on the theme of dreams and reality?

Ye Mi: We see that some mundane things matter to a person because of their particular meaning to him/her. I once met an old man who went overseas for his studies before 1949. Instead of his diploma, he kept some rubbish he picked up on the road, which he cherished more than the degree. We might say he was sick or perverted, but who can say for sure that the rubbish was truly rubbish? A thing is the best in the eyes of those who like it, and this turns the mundane into magic. In writing, as long as it is what the characters love, it must be connected to dreams, and thus it becomes beautiful. And anything beautiful can only be appreciated with distance.

Jin Ying: When I read your stories before, I sensed the raging torrents underneath the smooth surface, and found the gap between the detached tone and the seemingly absurd plot particularly intriguing. But "Peach Blossom" conveys a different message, namely, choosing to seek and believe in something true and beautiful despite various lies in the world. This detachment is seen in both the words and the mindset. The techniques also break away from the confinement of the plot, with a flavor of prose. Does it have something to do with your mentality as you grow older? You said in an interview, "I no longer intend to be aggressive, so I need to find a different language of expression." Is this "different language" that found in "Peach Blossom" ?

Ye Mi: When I was writing "Peach Blossom," I was moving from the city to the northern part of a small town near Lake Taihu, where frogs' loud croaks would awaken anyone who was sleeping soundly. But living there, one's mind is at peace. With no street lights in the residential area, the moonlight seems particularly bright. When it rains in the daytime, one may sit on the steps in front of the house, enjoying flying birds and fallen leaves over a hot cup of tea. Writing born of this circumstance has to be detached.

Jin Ying: In your "Huamatou (Flowery Pier Town)" series, there are a variety of talented, romantic people: the merciful character Ai, the janitor Old Wu, and the passenger Su. Lies and goodwill, dreams and reality are all presented there. For the "Flowery Pier Town," do you have a long-term writing plan to depict a distinctive rural picture with an array of characters?

Ye Mi: Yes. In 2008 when I moved to rural areas, I started to "build" a village inhabited by different people with different experiences, hence the "Flowery Pier Town," with Baiju Bay, Mount Xianglu, Peach Blossom Ferry Crossing, Blue Lake, Bailu Village, and others. Then I found it was far from being enough. There needed to be a corresponding city, hence the old city "Wuguo," with all the urban characters. By the time I wrote *A Sketch Book of Romance*, I naturally linked Wuguo City, Baiju Bay, and Flowery Pier Town with those villages as the geographical backdrop of the stories. I did this, not for seeking difference, but for convenience. It was easier to summarise in terms of culture and customs. When I portray characters in future writing, it will feel like I am telling stories of some old acquaintances, helping the reader to see characters exposed to a particular culture.

Jin Ying: This year is the 20th anniversary of the first publication of your works in 1994. During these two decades, your writing, in terms of number and theme, has not changed with general writing trends. Your writings are primarily novellas or short stories, with just two novels, including *A Sketch Book of Romance*. In a time when longer works have gained popularity, writers like you who are particular about the number of words have become increasingly fewer. A writer usually has a standard for his/her writing. What kind of writing meets your standard? What is your state of mind when you're writing?

You've never been an "attention-seeking" writer, but since the publication of *The Sun Also Rises*, more readers have turned their attention from the adapted movie to your work. How does this kind of attention impact your life and writing? Which leads me to quite a general question: what prompts you to write? What does literary writing mean to you?

Ye Mi: From the day I moved away from the city, I have been looking for something that has less to do with my writing than with my life. Simply put, what do I want? At the beginning of my writing career, I had simple motives, so why did I feel lost and overwhelmed along the way? People get to know themselves best when they are alone. I mentioned in one of my essays that I was quite alone when living here, as there were only two families in the entire neighborhood—me and a businessman. We lived at the opposite end of the neighborhood and felt world apart. Sometimes when I went to bed at night, I was suddenly aware that I hadn't talked to a single person throughout the day, nor the day before. When I got up the next morning, I would go to the vegetable market to chat with the peddlers. After six years of such life, I have eventually recognized that I'm simply a piece of grass, ordinary but resilient. Having understood myself, I have learnt to take things easy. Writing is to write about oneself, and has nothing to do with others.

As for my standard of stories, I suppose it is to write my own words in an entirely unrestricted circumstance. But is this goal attainable? As for what literary writing means to me, I came to realize not long ago that I was destined to be a homeless child, and it is literature that takes me in.

Jin Ying: You wrote in your stories about sitting and observing the growth of plants and the differences between urban and rural dew. And most of the titles of your stories are connected with flowers, such as Flowery Pier Town, Peach Blossom Ferry Crossing, and Nianhua (Flower-picking) Bridge. I guess you're a plant and nature lover in real life. You retreated to a pastoral life, and you stayed alone at Taihu Lake for six years to write this novel. Six years is not a short period, and most busy people today would find that unthinkable. During those six years, has your attitude towards life, writing, and literature changed according to your solitary life? When you chose to live in rural areas, did you plan to engage in writing? Could you describe your daily routine now?

Ye Mi: When I chose to live in the rural areas, I intended to rest and relax, as I was in bad health back then, suffering from insomnia, forgetfulness, heart palpitations, fatigue, anemia, and a lack of vitality. My goal was to be physically and mentally healthy. In those six years, I learnt to grow vegetables and plant trees, as well as to handle flowers, birds, and fish. Like a farming woman, I was physically and mentally fit. When writing now, I feel my words are more powerful than before. But I don't quite like the place anymore; it is getting too noisy and bustling, with no frogs' croaking, no rice paddies, and even fewer vegetable fields. At night, bright electric lights have dimmed the moonlight. I have no idea where I can move to instead—perhaps some isolated island, as I wish.

Culture & Heritage

The Essentials of Chinese Calligraphy

Yang Haocheng / 杨昊成

Consisting of three parts, viz., Evolution, Aesthetics, and Technique, this paper is an elementary introduction of Chinese calligraphy to an outsider or anyone who might be interested in this abstract form of art. In Part One, a brief history of the evolution of the five major scripts, i.e., the seal script, the clerical script, the model script, the walking script, and the running/cursive script, is introduced. In Part Two, the paper addresses the question of the appreciation of Chinese calligraphy from three aspects: strokes, character formation, and composition, mentioning in passing the cultivation of artistic taste. Discussed in the last part are the "four treasures of the study," the correct way of brush holding, the "eight components of the character *yong,*" and the imitating of masters' models, etc.

I Evolution

Roughly speaking, the history of Chinese calligraphy is as long as Chinese civilization itself. As the burgeoning of an upcoming full-blossomed art of calligraphy, pictograph is a crude, primeval, direct, but most true-to-nature portrayal of both images and ideas, the function of which is not unlike the primitive cave paintings in Lascaux of France or Altamira of Spain, both well-known in the history of Western art. It's much of guesswork about exactly who invented China's first pictograph or picture-writing. It is generally believed that a certain four-eyed man Cang Jie (仓颉), the official recorder to the semi-mythical Yellow Emperor (黄帝), styled as Xuanyuan (轩辕), was the first to observe the marks of birds' talons and animals' footprints on the ground, the shapes of shadows cast by trees, etc., and was thus inspired to engrave the rough representations of their forms on a sort of notched-sticks (书契)[1], which was similar to the English tally. These picture-writings were gradually modified into the very first characters of the Chinese language. They are, understandably, our ancestors' ingenious capriccios; subject to

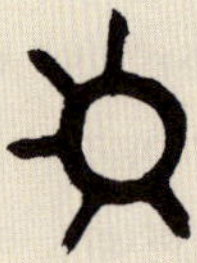

Fig.1a *Ri* (日), The sun

Fig.1b *Yue* (月), The moon

Fig.1c *Zhou* (舟), Boat

Fig.1d *Hu* (壶), Pot

Fig.1e *Qiu* (囚), Prisoner

Fig.1f *Ming* (明), Bright (The sun and the moon together stand for brightness.)

Fig.1g *Zhi* (至), Reach (The upper part indicates a bird, and the lower, land: A bird flying to land means "reach.")

change, they had no set rules in and for themselves which were later to regulate and standardize the writing of Chinese characters. A few examples here might give the reader a visual impression of what the earliest forms of Chinese calligraphy looked like (Fig.1)

With the passage of time, the ancients soon came to find that the few crude characters were quickly failing to meet the pressing needs to record the increasingly complicated human affairs. More characters were formed as a result but still very much at the mercy of our ancestors' caprice. By the 17th century B.C. when the Shang Dynasty came into being, these characters began to show up *en masse* on animal bones and particularly on tortoise shells. They were engraved with a needle-like knife on these hard surfaces which were used for oracle purposes. They came to be known as *jia gu wen* (甲骨文), the shell-and-bone script, or simply oracle-bone script.

By 800 B.C. an imperial amanuensis by the name of Zhou (籀) had drawn up a system of characters based upon the previous shell-and-bone script. They were called *gu wen* (古文), or directly after his name, *Zhou wen* (籀文). History by then had developed from the Shang to the Zhou Dynasty which witnessed a sudden, miraculous surge of bronze vessels. Most of the *Zhou wen* were now engraved on this newly discovered metal which was supposed and did in effect prove to be more durable than animal bones and tortoise shells. They were called *jin wen* (金文), or metal script. And because bronze was almost always used to cast bells or vessels for ancestor worshipping services both on national and tribal or clan occasions, the characters engraved thereupon were also called *zhong ding wen* (钟鼎文), the bell-and-quadripod/tripod script. Later philologists and calligraphers picked up a new name for it, *da zhuan* (大篆), the great seal. It had a quaint beauty and charm of solidness, dignity, and irregularity, and though hardly legible even to many professional calligraphers of today, is still practiced by a few hands for the sheer beauty of its forms.

Pleasing to the eye as it was, the great seal was developed in a most casual and unrestrained vein so that when Qin Shihuang (秦始皇) eventually conquered the warring states and ascended the throne as China's First Emperor who had achieved the country's unification, the first time ever in her history, he felt it urgent not only to centralize the state power, but also to unify, regulate, and standardize such things as the currency, measurements, and ways of writing which had run so diverse and divergent that they were almost out of control, constituting a lurking threat to his newly-unified state. So following the great seal, *xiao zhuan* (小篆), the small seal, came into existence in answer to the call of both the Emperor and the times. The small seal was of a much more unified and regular form than that of the great seal and easily recognizable. The person who was responsible for this style was Li Si (李斯), the First Emperor's prime minister. Li developed an easy way of character formation in which he simply combined, with due modifications, the existing pictographs with a phonetic element. In this way he produced over 3,000 characters. Other scholars added to his repertoire using his method so that by 200 A.D. the number had risen up to over 10,000. This marked an important turning point in the development of Chinese civilization, the significance of which went well beyond the realm of calligraphy itself. Thenceforward, learning could be more easily disseminated with a standard script. All the irregularities were dropped and a dazzling array of variants of ancient scripts was unified into one. On this basis there evolved all the upcoming scripts and styles of Chinese calligraphy.

Li Si is credited with the honor of the Father of the Seal Sript and yet only two engravings, *Langya Tai* (琅琊台) and *Yishan Bei* (峄山碑), can be ascribed to him with authenticity. But in the course of the twenty-odd centuries even these two were severely damaged. Both are records of the feats and distinctions of the First Emperor who, as an excessively superstitious man, made more than one long journey from his capital Xi'an all the way eastward to the allegedly holy mountains in the east to look for elixir. On these journeys the Prime Minister was always in the Emperor's company. The famous *Yishan Bei*, a memorial engraved on Mount Yi in present Shandong Province has been looked up to as a masterpiece of the small seal representative of Li's style. [2] (Fig.2) Readers are advised to take note of the uniform size of the characters, the even thickness of the strokes, the smooth curve, and the beautiful balance of the structure. Incidentally, *zhuan ke* (篆刻), or seal-carving, which has developed into an independent art form, is closely related to the seal script, both in character formation and overall design. A seal-carver has to be first of all a good hand at this style of

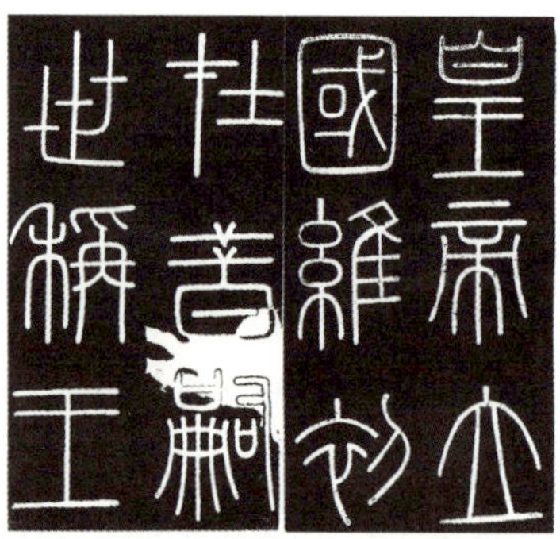

Fig.2 *Yishan Bei* (part), a copy of Li Si's hand, by Xu Xuan (徐铉) of the Southern Tang Dynasty

calligraphy.

Understandably, the seal script is slow and difficult to write. It takes patience, effort, and good control of breath. As the pace of life quickened, people simply couldn't afford all that was required of this laborious script. Indeed, they had to engrave or carve with a knife rather than write with a brush. It was at this historical juncture that a brand-new style of Chinese calligraphy was to be born in answer to the needs of the common people. But its very birth has an interesting story to tell. A petty official serving in the court somehow offended the First Emperor and was sentenced to ten years in Yunyang Prison in the then capital Xi'an. With seemingly endless days to kill and virtually nothing to do, this man, Cheng Miao (程邈), developed a keen interest in calligraphy and brooded over a new style of writing. For he came to find that *zhuan shu* was too cumbersome and inconvenient a tool to wield and no good for practical purposes. Cheng managed to simplify and modify the strokes in that all the curved lines which were characteristic of *zhuan shu* were straightened up. He had produced altogether about 3,000 characters using this method which I call *fang hua* (方化), or squarization. It's interesting to note, incidentally, that because of his innovation, Cheng Miao was released from prison before he had served his sentence; in fact he was even promoted to a higher position than he used to hold. But ironically enough, his new style was denied an official, formal, dignified status that the established *zhuan shu* had long been enjoying. Instead, it was given a fairly lowly name *li shu* (隶书), the clerical script, or *zuo shu* (佐书), the assistant script, considered to be fit for use only by the clerks, secretaries, or petty officials. But later developments of calligraphy show all too clearly that *li shu* became increasingly popular with the entire population and was to step by step replace *zhuan shu* as the officially recognized and propagated script of the Han Dynasty. However, the denomination *li shu* itself continues to the present day.

Culturally speaking, the Han Dynasty is one of China's golden ages. As far as calligraphy is concerned, Han was not only the first peak but marked a revolutionary turn in that virtually all the major styles of Chinese calligraphy were by then firmly established. All the dynasties to follow, be it Tang, Song, Yuan, Ming or Qing, were merely further developments, improvements, and branching out into new routes. The sudden leap forward in the art of calligraphy was largely due to the improvement of the writing tool. The discovery of the wondrous qualities of the writing brush made this calligraphic revolution possible.[3] Dipped into the black ink, *mao bi* (毛笔), a cluster of hair in the shape of a cone snugly fixed into one end of a slender bamboo or reed tube, was found to be a wonder maker. With a little practice, any writer was able to produce some unexpected miraculous effects: The strokes could be easily shaped into varying thickness with each slight pressing or raising of the working hand, and even an unnoticeable turn of either the fingers, the wrist or the arm would render the strokes steady or hasty, heavy or light, dry or wet, square or circular. Compared to the earlier knife which was an indispensable tool when working on hard and solid materials such as bone, shell, stone, and bronze, brush was undoubtedly much quicker and more convenient to wield, thus becoming a more eloquent and fluent instrument to express the writer's craftsmanship, talents, and very soon, emotions and sentiments. The poetry of calligraphy was greatly enhanced and it was much easier for calligraphers to add ornamental elements or touches to the characters which were till then chiefly treasured for their utilitarian values of, say, recording history.

Although Han witnessed maturity of all the major styles of calligraphy, the Dynasty has long been associated chiefly with the clerical script. This was not only because that this particular script had never since been surpassed by any of the following ages, but that the other scripts, namely, *kai shu* (楷书), the model script,[4] *xing shu* (行书), the walking script, and *cao shu* (草书), the running or cursive script and a number of their variants, were yet to reach relative perfection in the hands of a galaxy of masters, notably those from the Jin, Tang, and Song dynasties.

Much to our regret and puzzlement, however, among the numerous stelae and their rubbings in the clerical script left from Han, none was signed so that we shall never be able to know the names of the writers of those marvelous calligraphic works. Cai Yong (蔡 邕), recognized as the most outstanding calligrapher of Han, was only recorded and praised in his contemporaries' words and books, and yet no authentic examples of his hand have survived.

As its denomination suggests, the model script, on which our present-day printing style is based, as can be easily seen, has been looked upon as a model set for practitioners of calligraphy to follow. For although much more simplified as compared to *zhuan shu*, the

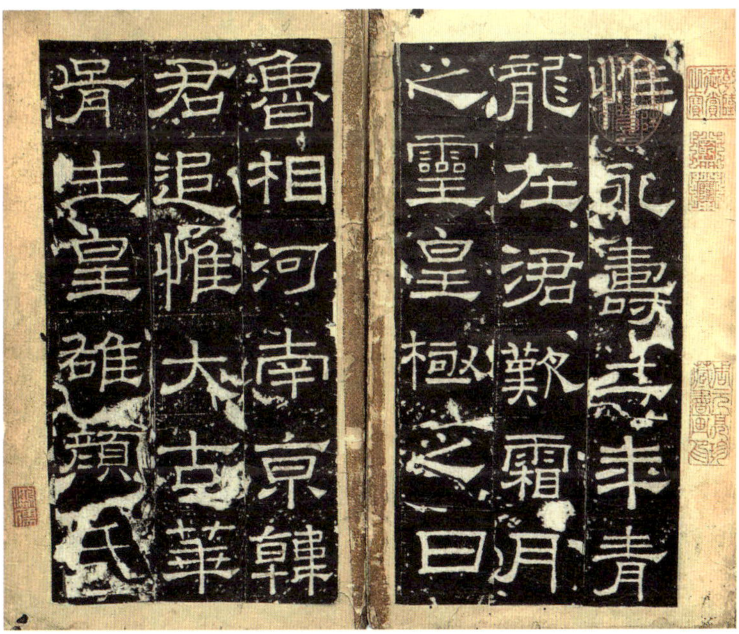

Fig.3 *Liqi Bei* (礼器碑, part) of the East Han Dynasty. Note the horizontal strokes which are typical *can tou yan wei*, or "the head of a silkworm and the tail of a swallow."

clerical script still keeps some decorative elements of which the most representative one is the so-called *can tou yan wei* (蚕头燕尾), or "the head of a silkworm and the tail of a swallow." (Fig.3) For practical use, graceful, ornamental strokes such as this one ask for pruning and modification until a new script can be found which is to be the happy marriage of aesthetics and functionality. Such a combination was found in *kai shu*.

Almost all scholars agree that *kai shu* reached its apogee in the Tang Dynasty when it boasted three of the four universally recognized *kai shu* masters, Yan Zhenqing (颜真卿), Liu Gongquan (柳公权), and Ouyang Xun (欧阳询), the fourth one Zhao Mengfu (赵孟頫) coming some time later, between the Southern Song and Yuan dynasties. But in fact, as early as the Jin Dynasty *kai shu* had already reached its full maturity and gained a quaint beauty under the brush tip of Zhong You (钟繇), popularly considered to be the patriarch of *kai shu*. Then we had Wang Xizhi (王羲之), a real gentleman, an aristocrat, a poetic prose writer, but above all an agglomerator of virtually all the basic scripts of Chinese calligraphy, the indisputable "Prince of Calligraphy" who was not to be surpassed till this day by any calligrapher in the generations after him. Li Shiming (李世民), known as Emperor Taizong of the Tang Dynasty, one of the very few sage emperors in Chinese history, reputed for both his martial prowess and literary talents, and no mean calligrapher himself, compared Wang to an unapproachable lofty mountain whereas all the other calligraphers were mere hillocks and mounds. I'll come back to Wang in a moment.

It's generally agreed that *kai shu* enjoyed two prosperous periods, the Wei and Tang dynasties. The Tang masters mentioned above had an overwhelming influence upon literally all beginners of calligraphy. Their reputation and status remained unchallenged for over 800 years until Qing when a group of scholar calligraphers represented by Bao Shichen

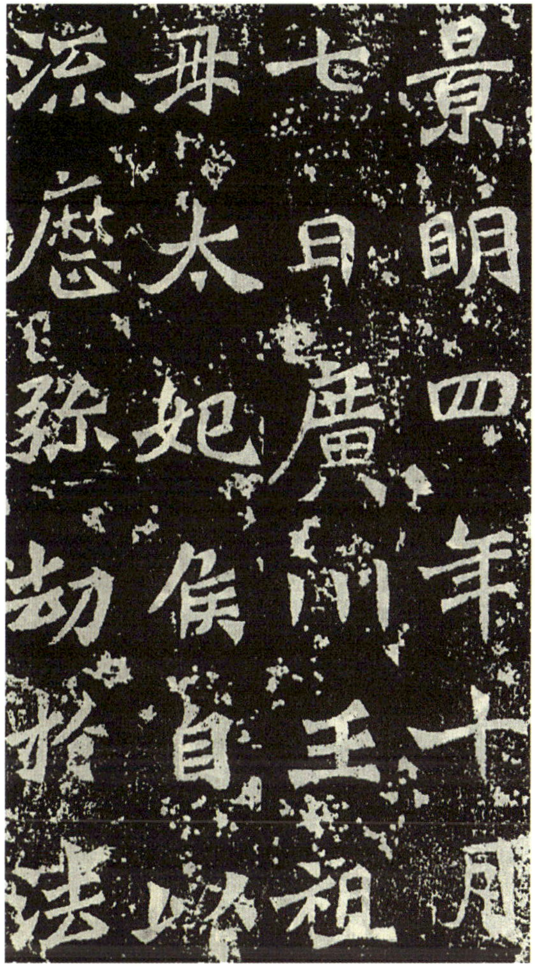

Fig.4 One of the *Twenty Pieces in Longmen* (part)

(包世臣) began to voice with good justification and abundant evidence their growing boredom and dissatisfaction with and strong aversion to Tang *kai* (*kai shu* of the Tang Dynasty) which, in their eyes, had been going downhill all along until it had lost its early features such as life, vigor, solidness, naiveté, crude and unaffected beauty, and charm of irregularity and unusual structuring. For such desirable features, Bao and his followers harked back to the Wei and the Northern Wei period in particular, which abounded in aesthetically powerful works such as the *Twenty Pieces in Longmen* (龙门二十品).[5] (Fig.4) Calligraphically, therefore, Qing was called by quite a few scholars and calligraphers "the Era of Revitalization." Such an argument was glorified, carried on, and further developed by some contemporary scholars and calligraphers, notable exemplifiers of whom include Kang Youwei (康有为), Zeng Xi (曾熙), Li Ruiqing (李瑞清), Yu Youren (于右任), Hu Xiaoshi (胡小石), Xu Beihong (徐悲鸿), to name only a few.

Teachers of calligraphy usually advise their pupils to start with *kai shu* and then move on to *xing shu* and *cao shu*. They like to compare *kai shu* to "a person standing," arguing, "If one cannot stand, how can he walk? If he cannot walk, how can he run?" [6] One cannot say, however, that *xing shu* and *cao shu* are derived from *kai shu*, for both were actually created before the real *kai shu* was established.[7] Zhang Huaiguan (张怀瓘), one of the best known calligraphic critics and theoreticians of Tang, attributed the invention of *xing shu* to Liu Desheng (刘德升) of the Later Han period,[8] though Liu is not regarded by most as a good calligrapher.

While *kai shu* is an essential prerequisite to a calligraphic career, most writers soon feel inclined to *xing su*, for although both its strokes and patterns are designed and executed in each minute detail as those of *kai shu*, they are, after all, written in a quicker way. The characters are still written separately, one by one, but strokes within each character are mostly joined together so that a certain fluency and greater expressiveness are achieved. It comes as no big surprise then that this more eloquent and artistic script easily replaces the rigid, formal *kai shu* as the most popular script with calligraphers. Utilitarianistically speaking, on the other hand, *xing shu* is comparatively easier and more convenient to write. It is also, perhaps without our own awareness, what our handwriting today is based upon. People never use *kai shu* to write each other or to keep notes in class, let alone *zhuan shu* or *li shu*, much as no Westerners will ever print in their correspondence or notebooks.

I will not burden my readers with those celebrated *xing shu* calligraphers throughout the ages because there are too many. I will content myself by simply

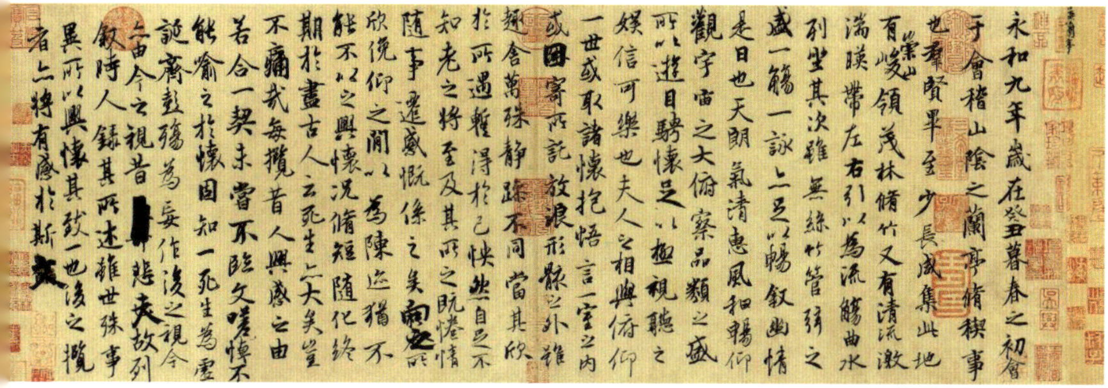

Fig.5 *Preface to the Collected Writings at the Orchard Pavilion Gathering*, a copy of Wang Xizhi's hand, by Feng Chengsu (冯承素) of the Tang Dynasty

calling your attention to the biggest names, Wang Xizhi, Yan Zhenqing, and Su Dongpo (苏东坡), the authors of "Preface to the Collected Writings at the Orchard Pavilion Gathering" (兰亭集序), "Manuscript in Memory of Ji Ming, My Nephew" (祭侄季明文稿), and "A Poem Composed in Huangzhou on the Cold-food Day " (黄州寒食诗), reputed to be the "Numbers One, Two, and Three *Xing Shu* in the World." The most famous and legendary of the three is of course the Number One, but part of its fame is derived from the story of how nearly three centuries after it was written (353 A.D.), through tricks and plots, it got into the hands of the Tang Emperor Taizong who had such a crush on it that he had it interred with him in Zhao Ling (昭陵), his huge mystery-and-treasure-ridden mausoleum in Xi'an.[9] (Fig.5)

As the "Prince of Calligraphy," Wang Xizhi is an incredibly versatile genius. Comparatively speaking, however, Wang is best known for his *xing shu* and *cao shu.* But among the alleged dozens of Wang's calligraphic works in existence today, only one, popularly known as *Kuai Xue Shi Qing Tie* (快雪时晴帖), is unanimously considered to be genuine. It is one of the three rarities hoarded by the mad amateur calligrapher Emperor Qian Long of the Qing Dynasty, who used it to name one of his studies *San Xi Tang* (三希堂), the Hall of Three Rarities, the other two genuine pieces being *Zhong Qiu Tie* (中秋帖) by his

7th son Wang Xianzhi (王献之), or Wang Jr., and *Bo Yuan Tie* (伯远帖) by Wang Xun (王珣), his nephew.

Strictly speaking, *zhang cao* (章草), the earlier form of *cao shu* came in between *li shu* and *kai shu*. It's hard to pinpoint the inventor of *zhang cao*; some records pick out Cai Yong, others Du Cao (杜草), and still others even argue for the Han emperor Zhang (章帝). The word *zhang* means "essay" in this contest, and *cao* is "rough" or "hasty." Put it simply, the two words combined mean "rough essay," suggesting a draft written in a hasty, sketchy manner. But later, both literati and calligraphers found a quaint beauty of a sort in itself and some even went on to specialize in this unique way of forming characters. New and more audacious experiments were made on *zhang cao* which, however hurriedly written, was still easily legible, not only because the characters were independent of one another, but because the strokes within each word were hardly joined together as those in the later *cao shu* known as *jin cao*(今草), the modern running script. Different from *xing shu*, the walking, strokes forming a character were now so simplified and integrated that they sometimes appeared to be done in one single brush stroke. Some radicals went still further; their uncurbed force and flying rapidity in wielding the brush were capable of producing a continuous line linking several characters all together. In fact, an entire piece could be done in one stroke and such a piece is justifiably called *kuang cao*(狂草), or the "crazy cursive script." Representatives of *kuang cao* are, besides Wang Xizhi, Zhang Xu (张旭) and Huaisu (怀素), of Tang, famed as "*dian zhang zui su*," (颠张醉素) or "the crazy Zhang and the drunken Su." (Fig.6) It is very important to note, however, that both *jin cao* and *kuang cao* have *cao fa* (草法), a set of established rules designed for beginners to follow. The rationale is simple: If each writer is to go his own way, what one produces will be Latin, or, in a popular Chinese parlance, *tian shu* (天书), "writings from the Heaven," to another. It absolutely is a misconception

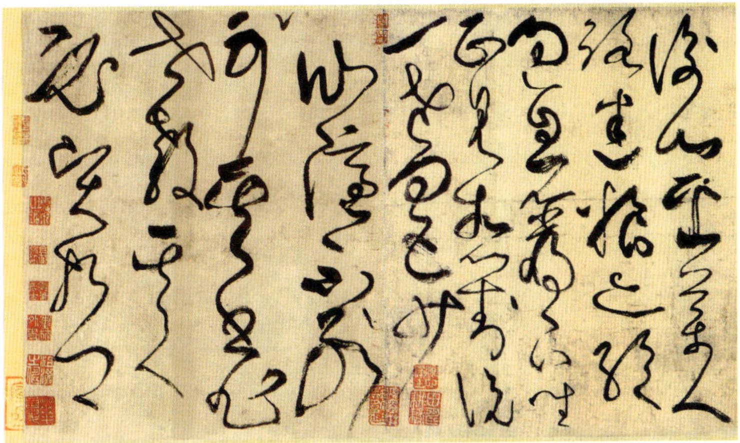

Fig.6 Four ancient poems (part) in the "crazy cursive script" by Zhang Xu of the Tang Dynasty

that *cao shu* is a careless, slipshod, and slovenly script and any one can do it if he has "guts" enough to write his characters in a dazzling, crazy way. The "craziness" in *cao shu* almost always refers to the mood and emotions conveyed in the work by the writer and not just those rash and mad strokes dashed onto some surface. It takes years of preparation in *zhuan, li, kai, xing* scripts and patient and strenuous practice in *cao fa* before one becomes a qualified *cao shu* calligrapher.

II Aesthetics

"In China, perhaps more than anywhere else, calligraphy came to be regarded as a fine art, practiced by men of education and social eminence... Each piece of calligraphy was thought to reflect its writer's character and feelings. The strength, balance, and flow of the strokes made with a highly pliable hair brush were believed to convey the calligrapher's moral and psychological make-up as well as his momentary emotions." [10] This is largely true with professionals; with an amateur, even if it's an adequately educated Chinese, it is a different story. An outsider may find it such a demanding job to truly appreciate a piece of calligraphic work. His puzzlement and bewilderment are very similar to those who stand in front of a Western abstract Expressionist painting. He might feel pleased with the form, but he doesn't know, if he is honest enough, what exactly makes it pleasing. What is good calligraphy and how to discriminate between the good and the bad are indeed difficult questions to answer. To speak good Chinese or fluently read a Chinese text is one thing, and to be able to "write a beautiful hand," as the Chinese like to say, is quite another. Ask any foreigner in China or even those who have become Chinese citizens and who have been living in this land throughout their lives, I bet they will nod a yes. For the "making of a Chinese is one of the world's most demanding and impressive of all cultural accomplishments. Chineseness is not something that you can just grow up with and absorb naturally." To "metamorphose into a complete Chinese" or "to become a complete *Chinese* Chinese," one has to "deliberately engage in a tremendous amount of hard work over a period of many years." [11] And then there are different levels of *Chineseness*: Being able to speak good Chinese is one, preferring a cup of Longjin tea to a mug of strong coffee is another; being sufficiently skilled at reading and writing is a great leap forward, and "writing a beautiful hand" with a brush would add the final touch to the genuine *Chineseness*.

But what a challenge to attain that level! While acknowledging calligraphy to be one of the most distinguishing features of Chinese culture, an outsider, be it a Chinese or an alien, will, in general, still find this "art of the line" exotic, esoteric, elusive, and mysterious. Chiang Yee (蒋彝), one of the pioneers in introducing traditional aspects of Chinese art to the West in English,[12] tries to unveil the mystery of Chinese calligraphy. But let's see if the mystery is removed: "Calligraphy is not a symmetrical arrangement of conventional shapes. It is like the coordinated movements of a skillfully composed dance; movements that include impulse, momentum, momentary poise and the interplay of active forces combined to form a balanced whole." [13] Chiang's succinct definition of the aesthetic of Chinese calligraphy "is simply this: that a beautiful form should be beautifully executed." [14] Such a definition, if it can be called one, easily invites criticism so that even Sir Herbert Reed who praises Chiang's English treatise *Chinese Calligraphy* and contributes a preface to it for "its significance for the general philosophy of art, and more particularly by its bearing on certain aspects of modern art," [15] challenges it, out of good will, no doubt, by writing: "But the aesthetic of Chinese painting is simply that too; and so is the aesthetic of Chinese sculpture or Chinese pottery. I would say that this is a universal principle of all art..." [16]

To do Mr Chiang justice, the quotes here together with all the other contents in his treatise are, comparatively speaking, still simple, clear, concrete, and comprehensible. In fact there have been countless essays, poems, and books written on calligraphy ever since it became an independent art, and the majority of the theories and discussions are, to our greatest agony, nebulous and abstruse, woven in flowery language and shrouded in mystery. Animism is always shown to be at work when strokes constituting a Chinese character are compared to natural objects so that "*heng* (横), or a horizontal line, is like a formation of clouds stretching a thousand miles; *dian* (点), or a dot, is like a rock falling from a high peak; *pie* (撇), or a stroke sweeping with a little curve from up right to down left, is like the sharp edge of a sword or the horn of a rhinoceros; *ge* (戈), or a stroke moving with a little curve from up left to down right ending with an up-turned sharp point, is like a hook with great force; *shu* (竖), or a vertical line, is like a dry vine thousands of years old; *na* (捺), a stroke in near opposition to *pie*, is like a wave surging forth or a flying cloud cracking rumbles of thunder; and *wan* (弯), an angular curve ending with a hook, is like the sinews and joints of a strong crossbow, at once pliable and full of tension." [17] These time-honored doctrines popularly known as *qi miao* (七妙), or the "seven mysteries," were formulated by Madam Wei (卫夫人), Wang Xizhi's aunt as well as his first teacher of calligraphy. Madam Wei also used such physiological images as "flesh," "bone," and "sinew" to describe ideal or sick strokes: "In the writing of those who are skillful in giving strength of stroke, the characters are 'bony' ; in the writing of those who are not skillful in giving strength of stroke, the characters are 'fleshy.' Writing that has a great deal of bone and very little meat is called 'sinewy writing,' and writing that is full of flesh and weak bone is called 'piggy writing.' A writing that is powerful and sinewy is divine; a writing that has neither power nor sinews is like an invalid." [18]

To be very frank, I quite doubt the intelligibility of all these similes and metaphors in spite of their vividness and luring images. Indeed, would they mean anything to an outsider? I never hold an optimistic view towards the slightest possibility of Chinese calligraphy being accepted with real honesty by any Chinese without special training or actual experience. With an alien, it is even more utopian and hopeless. I know this all too well from my twenty-plus years of teaching foreign students both home and abroad. While all practitioners of Chinese calligraphy are required to spend at least a couple of years on each of the five major scripts, *zhuan, li, kai, xing, cao*, faithfully and persistently copying and imitating the models of established ancient masters, my foreign friends would most of them tell me that they were ready to move on to a new script a few minutes after dragging their clumsy brush on the paper, laboriously working on their self-claimed *kai shu*. Half an hour or so later you would catch them flaunting their "crazy cursive" already! Years after years of patient practice of the same script, hundreds of times of meticulous imitating of a few lines written by a master hand, or ecstasy and intoxication over the beauty of a single line or the unique structuring of a character would appear to be not much different from madness in their eyes. So to me, every effort would avail to nil if one does not pick up a brush and actually begin to write. Real, intimate, and preferably daily contact with the "four treasures of the study" will, believe me, sooner or later lead you across the threshold of the palace of the art of calligraphy, where you can not only expect to gain, bit by bit, an entry into the innermost recesses of that sensitive and exquisite Chinese soul, but very likely, end up an incorrigible addict to the formerly recondite and repelling genre of Chinese art.

But still, there are a few tips for both practitioners and would-be connoisseurs of Chinese calligraphy. When facing a piece of calligraphy, we generally look for three things, namely, *dian hua* (点画), or the stroke; *jie zi* (结字), or the structuring of a character; and *zhang fa* (章法), or the composition of the whole piece. Each succeeding one is built on the one which precedes it, i.e., *jie zi* is built on *dian hua*, and *zhang fa* is built on *jie zi*. For writing strokes the correct way of moving the brush is of utmost importance. It has always been maintained that the entire aesthetics of Chinese calligraphy is really the product of brush movement. And brush movement, according to Zhao Mengfu, the most famous calligrapher and painter of the Yuan Dynasty, never changes. It's a misconception, however, that only one single way of moving the brush is correct and all others are wrong. But one can never over emphasize the importance of *zhong feng yong bi* (中锋用笔), a brush movement with its tip moving along the middle of the stroke. *Zhong feng yong bi* is required of all strokes, particularly those in *zhuan shu, li shu,* and *kai shu*. Such strokes are considered to be filled with life and strength. If you hold the paper up to the light you'll detect a darker streak running down the middle of the stroke, the ink around it being lighter, or, "bone" in the center with "flesh" and "sinews" girdling it. However, because the brush is soft and pliable, it is in effect impossible to always keep its tip faithfully stay in the central track. One has to readjust the hair from time to time in the process of which the brush is oftentimes found to be in a slanting position. This is termed *ce feng* (侧锋), the slanting hair which, although against the predominant rule of *zhong feng yong bi*, brings about some unexpected artistic effects such as light and graceful strokes, and when wielded quickly, even *fei bai* (飞 白), or "flying whites," a sort of vigorous, impressive strokes with hollow lines within. One can easily imagine, with the suppleness of the bush moving along the surface of the miraculously porous and absorbent special Chinese paper, *xuanzhi* (宣 纸), what an infinite variety of strokes each slight turn, twist, pressing, and raising of the brush tube could produce! One is sure to feast his eyes with the abstract beauty of the line with such qualities as "force, suppleness, reserved strength, exquisite tenderness, swiftness, neatness, massiveness, ruggedness, and restraint or freedom." [19] Here the meaning means little, if anything, and "the lines and forms are appreciated in and for themselves." [20]

It is equally important to note that calligraphy is dynamic and not static. Its life and beauty lie in movement. Calligraphic strokes are, therefore, appreciated for their pure "beauty of momentum," [21] written in a confidant, powerful way, defying any correction or touching up. Any strokes that are "drawn," "painted," or written in a hesitant way are considered dead. Mr Chiang has a good comparison between calligraphy and skating: "The 'push-off' of a stroke provides the impetus, as with a skater, and the hand follows through and governs the movement exactly as the skater controls his 'figure'. And just as a skater who loses control of his body either falls or is thrown into an awkward posture, so bad handwriting is the result of a failure of the writer to find an equilibrium between himself and his brush." [22] And even more so with dancing: "In dancing there are certain recognized positions for hands, feet and head. They are not symmetrical postures, but points of equilibrium, variable with the figure of the dancer, which occur in the course of the movements. In calligraphy there are similar conventional positions for the strokes..."[23] Chiang asserts that "After some experience of writing one begins to feel a movement springing to life under the brush which is, as it were, spontaneous. It is present in even a single stroke or dot. The brush acts rhythmically, stretching to the left, drawing away to the right, turning, pirouetting, poising. The stroke responds to the slightest movement of the wrist and fingers or of the right elbow and arm. The sensation is really very like that aroused by a ballerina balancing upon one toe, revolving, leaping, and poising on the other toe. The same qualities are demanded of the writer."[24] (Fig.7)

While brush movement never changes, *jie zi*, or the structuring of a character, has never stopped changing. Chinese characters are known as *fang kuai zi* (方块字), or "square-shaped words." Never try to slight that invisible little square! That's a mini-cosmos in which possibilities and variations are virtually limitless. Each individual master hand has developed his own distinctive way of structuring characters so that different styles named after these powerful figures such as Wang *zi*, Yan *zi*, Liu *zi*, Ou *zi*, Su *zi*, Mi *zi*, Huang *zi*, Zhao *zi*, etc., are known. It is not uncommon, on the other hand, that an unrivaled, dominant figure can exert overwhelming influence on the calligraphic trend of a certain period. His unique way of character formation betrays, or defines, in a large measure, the ethos of an age. The Ming Dynasty, for example, bears the clear hallmark of Dong Qichang (董其昌), a calligrapher and painter, whose style was doggedly imitated by every aspiring writer of his time.

Fig.7 A comparison between calligraphy and dancing. The left character *sui* (遂), or "to satisfy," is in the running style of Wang Xizhi; the right dancing girl is a sketch by Chiang Yee.

Whether Dong's calligraphy is really worthy of the status and reputation he enjoyed is, however, another question. Of course one cannot say that *jie zi* alone decides everything; there are other factors at work. But it is an undeniable fact that the innumerable ways of character formation, theoretically at least, have promised the ever-changing, unpredictable physiognomy of Chinese calligraphy. This is also, incidentally, what is stunningly charming and visually stirring about this purest and the most abstract branch of all traditional forms of art in China.

In structuring a Chinese character the most important point to bear in mind is the principle of *shi* (势), or posture. Like strokes but now more stressing the relationship between strokes, *jie zi* should also be dynamic and not static: A horizontal line is never strictly level; a vertical line is hardly pen straight; nor is a square a perfect square, and geometric balance and symmetry are the last desired. Any character formation without posture would appear mechanic, wooden, arranged, and therefore dead. There is much to be argued for Bao Shichen and Kang Youwei who relentlessly criticized the Tang model script and all its later followers for their mechanic observance of the rigorous, "standard" rules for structuring each character. Both Bao and Kang believed that "there was no real *kai shu* after the Northern Wei period." [25] They went all out to advertise and advocate, both in theory and in practice, the study of the Wei stelae and their rubbings in which, they believed, lay all the spirit, value, and beauty of Chinese calligraphy. Their strongest argument was that Wei calligraphy boasted that amazing posture: Characters always seemed to be "on the point of toppling over, and yet always remain in balance." [26] Calligraphy of the Wei period was sweepingly in the model script, but the spontaneous application of *shi* is equally significant to all other scripts and styles.

For both *dian hua* and *jie zi*, a long period of concentrated and unremitting copying and imitating of the specimens of established ancient masters is compulsory.[27] For a beginner all that is to learn about the essentials of calligraphy can be obtained from *zi tie* (字帖), or copybooks. Sufficiently trained and the working hand well attuned to the call of the mind and the aesthetic mood of the moment, one is ready to experiment with a whole piece.

Zhang fa, or composition, is not too difficult a job if one has passed *cum laude* the stages of *dian hua* and *jie zi*. Composition is, to a certain degree, the magnification of *jie zi*, so to speak. One might as well compare an entire piece to one enlarged character in which all the comprising characters are its strokes. Likewise, *shi*, the posture, is stressed, but now it refers to the relationship not only between all the characters but that between characters and non-characters as well. The latter is usually referred to as the relationship between black and white, black being the actual characters and white the unoccupied space. An entire piece should look coherent, organic, knit together with posture, aesthetically reasonable, visually pleasing, and eye-catching in such a way that the more you look at it, the more you want to look and the more you harvest from your look.

Last but not least, a basic knowledge of the aesthetics of Chinese calligraphy gained from the actual experience may not be enough to make a first-rate calligrapher or a connoisseur. In the realm of art taste is an indispensable quality. Many believe that taste is not something that every one is blessed with. It is innate; he has it who happens to be born under a lucky star. Like genius it is grievously rare. But what a shame it would be if there were only a handful of those chosen few in this world! Taste can certainly be nurtured and cultivated. This is especially true of Chinese art. There is a preaching for traditional Chinese landscape painters which says, "Read ten thousand volumes and travel ten thousand *li*." Hardly has anyone ever achieved both, but it is always rewarding to try to take that challenge which aims at chastening the heart and broadening the mind. Artists working in other forms will benefit from this preaching also. In addition, genres in Chinese art are, unlike their Western counterparts, more or less interrelated so that calligraphy can inspire painting, poetry, sculpture, music, and even architecture and in turn be inspired by them. Chinese literati, artists, and scholars like to regard poetry, calligraphy, and painting as one entity, and the latter two, *shu hua* (书画), are in effect often referred to as "sister arts" sharing the same origin. At a higher and yet controversial level, the artist's personality and moral character are emphasized above all else.[28] Wen Zhenming (文徵明), one of the greatest Ming calligraphers and painters, believed that "If one's moral character is not high, his art will also lack style."[29] Su Dongpo's assertion that "All ailments can be cured, but vulgarity is incurable" is known to every student of art. All these admonitions and exhortations for artists hold true for good connoisseurs.

Ⅲ Technique

"Sharpen your tools first if you want your craft to be superb." The old saying is pretty much the same as: If you want to be a first-rate rider, get a Thorough-bred. The same is true of a calligrapher. The study of a traditional Chinese scholar and not necessarily that of a calligrapher or a painter is commonly equipped with an entire set of paraphernalia: Other than books put away in a wall of bookshelves or bookcases, there are always a couple of brushes, a few stacks of paper (for both practice and formal writing), an ink-stick, an ink-slab, a paper weight, a water-pot and a tiny spoon, a brush-hanger, a brush-stand, a brush-rest, some copybooks by ancient masters, etc. All these may be spread on a huge rectangular table specially made for the purpose of doing calligraphy, even as a hobby. To a scholar of the 21st century these facilities may appear to be no more than bric-a-brac or luxuries, but anyone who wants to try his hand at Chinese calligraphy, these "treasures" are the common desiderata. Perhaps he could do without the lesser items; many writers simply use their substitutes. But the brush and the paper are absolutely indispensable.

Chinese calligraphy becomes an independent form of art largely because of the writing brush. But it is important to note that the Chinese brush is entirely different from that used by a Western oil painter. Here the shape makes all the difference: The shape of a cone decides that all the hair, though of equal length, automatically falls into two parts, *zhu hao* (主毫), the major or the central hair, and *fu hao* (辅毫), the supporting hair. Inseparable from and complementing each other, strokes written with such a cone-shaped brush result in myriads of amazing, and very often unpredictable, forms pregnant with artistic effects. The hair is usually of three kinds, that of the goat, *yanghao* (羊毫) , which is soft and pliable; that of the weasel, *langhao* (狼毫), which is stiff and resilient; and the mixed, *jianhao* (兼豪), which is eclectic. It is tied together in small bunches and fixed into the end of a hollow tube usually made of bamboo or reed.

The Chinese paper for calligraphy again is vastly different from that commonly seen and used in the West. It does not have a stiff, shiny, and defying surface; instead it is porous, absorbent, and much softer. It responds to and cooperates with a wealth of exquisite brush movements. The two combined really work wonders and even a trying hand can attest to that. For beginners or for practicing, *mao bian zhi* (毛边纸) or *yuan shu zhi* (元书纸) are used; they are made of bamboo, rice stalks or the stems of reeds and have a relatively rough surface, unbleached and yellowish in color. For formal writing, a better kind, *xuan zhi* (宣纸),[30] is used. This paper is made of sandalwood, whitish in color and has a much finer texture whose niceties and subtleties are inexplicable to those without an actual contact.

Although brush and paper are the most essential requisites

for doing calligraphy, the two do not make the "four treasures of the study (文房四宝)," a household name in China, complete. The other two "treasures," the ink-stick and the ink-slab, are not as indispensable, but a sketchy introduction is still necessary.

The Chinese ink-stick is made of either *song yan* (松烟), the soot of burnt pine wood, or *you yan* (油烟), oil smoke (lampblack), collected and mixed with a kind of gum, rolled and beaten and hammered hundreds of times before being pressed into a mould to be taken out afterwards to dry to stone-hardness. *Song yan* is pure, somber black; *you yan* gives off a moderate luster. A calligrapher is supposed to contemplate and conceive the contours of the work he is about to create while he grinds the ink-stick calmly, evenly, over and over again in the ink-slab. But today most people simply make do with the prepared ink which is in liquid form and convenient to use and yet does not have the desired thickness or the amazing effect of the delicate hues.

The ink-slab is a flat stone with a hollow scooped out in the middle into which one fills a small amount of water to grind with the ink-stick. The texture of the stone has to be properly tight. There should be no tiny holes in it to nib away the ink, nor shall it be too tight like steel or glass so that the ink and the water are fended off altogether. Our ancestors say that rain water collected in a jar placed in the courtyard is most desirable; water from the well comes next. The amount of ink required to complete a piece of writing should be estimated at the outset. To be on the safe side, we usually grind a little more than we expect to use. To be obliged to grind more than one lot of ink for the same piece usually results in a noticeable variation of color and thickness. Moreover, if a considerable pause has to be made, fluency of the whole piece will be interrupted or affected. If the ink is ground too thickly, it will not run freely on the paper; if it is too thin, it will blot and expand into lines thicker than intended. It is always wise to make fresh ink for each piece of writing. Left on the stone, the gum curdles and the ink flows harshly and unevenly over the paper. Old ink is also apt to turn an unpleasant brownish color.[31] The ink-slab exists exclusively for the ink-stick, and because not many writers are using the ink-stick, ink-slabs are likewise marginalized though they make incredible treasures on the tables of some antiquarian collectors.

Now that the writer is equipped with the most essential tools for the job, he can come down to the real business of actual writing. But the correct way of holding the brush should first be grasped. Some even say that if one has learned to hold his brush correctly, he is half a calligrapher already. In fact each established master has his own comfortable way of holding the brush. For a beginner, however, one thing is absolute: He should never hold his brush as if he is holding a pen or a pencil. The brush should be strictly vertical, inclining neither to left nor right. The thumb and three other fingers should tightly grasp the tube on four sides, with the little finger in support. Five words are usually used to describe the different shapes of the five fingers and the parts they play in brush-holding, and they are *yan* (擫), to lift slantwise; *ya* (压), to press inward; *gou* (钩), to hook upward; *ge* (格), to fend off; and *di* (抵), to buttress. It is particularly important to note that none of the five fingers should touch the palm, otherwise the fist will be "locked" and it is literally impossible to move the brush around freely and produce the intended strokes, all the strength being concentrated in the palm and never reaching the brush's tip. Perhaps an illustration speaks better than all the words. (Fig.8)

Generally speaking, the distance between the fingers and

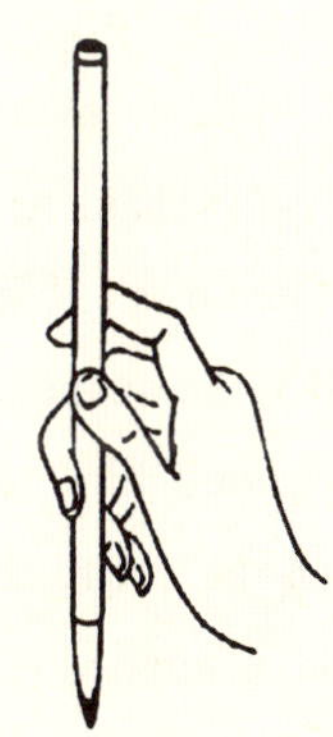

Fig.8 The correct way of brush holding

the hair depends on what scripts one is writing in. For *zhuan shu*, *li shu*, and *kai shu*, the proper distance is 1.3 inches; for *xing shu* and *cao shu*, 2.6 and 3.9 inches respectively. One can easily see that the further away from the hair, the more freedom the fingers enjoy and yet the more difficult it is to control the brush.

The size of the characters to be written largely governs the position of the wrist and the arm. For writing tiny characters one often uses *zhen wan* (枕腕), or the pillowed wrist, a position in which the right wrist rests on the left hand. On normal occasions *ping wan* (平腕), the level wrist, is used. For writing relatively bigger characters, *ti wan* (提腕), or the raised wrist, is preferred, for that position allows the brush to operate over a greater ambit. As the characters get even bigger, *xuan wan* (悬腕) or *xuan bi* (悬臂), the suspended wrist or suspended arm, a position in which the entire arm leaves the table, is applied. And finally when the characters get still bigger or the writer feels much too tied to his chair to adequately express his mood and emotions, he quits it and rises to his feet.

In writing each stroke, three most basic brush movements must be mastered: *Ti* (提), to raise; *an* (按), to press down; and *dun* (顿), to crouch. They are also the most workable ways to adjust the hair. As I have explained it in Part Two, *zhong feng yong bi* is the most desirable way of writing a stroke and yet the brush tip, because of the softness and pliability of the hair, will not always obediently move along the central track. The result is *pian feng* (偏 锋), the digressed hair, or *lou feng* (露锋), the exposed hair, which, to the Chinese eye, lack strength and vitality, *pian feng* resulting from dragging the brush with its "belly" rather than the tip along the paper, and *lou feng* showing uneven edges along the outlines of the strokes.

As mentioned at one point above, students of calligraphy are well advised to start with the model script; when the basic skills concerning both strokes and character formation are sufficiently grasped, they can move on to the other scripts in order of their preference. The aesthetic aspect of strokes and character formation have been discussed; as regards their techniques, a beginner is often told to practice *yong zi ba fa* (永字八法), or the "eight components of the character *yong*," [32] namesake of one of Wang Xizhi's books. The eight components forming *yong*, as shown in Fig.9, are: *ce* (侧), *le* (勒), *nu* (努), *ti* (趯), *ce* (策), *lüe* (掠), *zhuo* (啄), and *zhe* (磔). These terms, literally untranslatable, basically portray the poise and posture of the eight strokes intended. They also imply the different brush movements in writing these strokes. One is also required to learn to grasp the dynamically balanced structure of the character. Wang's theory in the book is abstruse and profound, difficult for beginners to comprehend, but it has been well interpreted in another namesake by a Qing scholar Li Puguang (李溥光), who extended the eight strokes to thirty-two. Li's elaboration is clear and helpful, but although his thirty-two strokes are fewer than Madam Wei's seventy-two, they are still too many for me to cover in this context. As it is, the more popular eight strokes of *yong* will suffice.

The solidification and perfection of the basic techniques, however, do not come from writing *yong* all the time. All those dreaming of writing a beautiful hand are urged without any exception to start by imitating the established masters, for as Kang Youwei asserted, "Those who cannot acquire the good qualities of old writers cannot put their talents into their own." [33] And in copying and imitating an ancient master, students are required to grasp not just his superficial forms but more importantly his idiosyncratic features and spirit, his unique

Fig.9 *Yong zi ba fa*, or the "eight components of the character *yong*"

style. It's usually considered a compliment if one's teacher or a professional comments on his work by being able to point out his inheritance, saying that his comes from Yan or Liu, Wang or Mi, although he almost always encourages the writer at the same time to develop his own unique style. He would be irked and ired if he fails to find anything ancestral in the learner's strokes. It is through such patient and sometimes boring imitating efforts that a practitioner gradually masters the correct way of writing strokes and the logical as well as the aesthetic way of structuring each character. Only when he has acquired the essence of a certain master is he encouraged to try someone else; stopping after a shallow dip or constantly shifting to anything new are reproved as a bad habit. One is also advised to scrutinize the copybooks and not just mechanically copy them one time after another. The subtleness of the original's strokes and the mystery of its composition very often do not just manifest themselves; they only come to the observant and searching eye. Having a master to teach or a professional friend to provide constant and specific help is a fortune that only falls on the lucky few. They can tell the writer from their own experience what to look for and what to avoid, thus leading him to bypass the pitfalls and traps so that he always moves forward in a correct and smooth way.

Even so, technically there are three stages to experience for all writers. First, the writer feels that he can make a copy which seems to him to be nearly as good as the original. This stage is a happy one, but now his eye is not yet trained well enough to enable him to perceive how far short his apprentice work really falls of the model. Further practice brings him to the second stage, when he realizes the evident inferiority of his work. This is so discouraging that sometimes the writer feels like putting away his brush and quitting altogether. However, progress has already been made without his own knowledge: Now he can not only detect his own weaknesses but has learned to appreciate the excellence of his model. This stage may drag on and on, but may also be transcended in a comparatively shorter period. Then coming as if it were a windfall, one day the writer does find that his copy is really not much different from the original. The frustration and boredom over the long imitation suddenly disappear and he is ecstatic to find that he has finally caught the spirit of the model and is now skilled enough to reproduce it. This is the third stage.[34]

Thus trained and baptized in the excellence of a wealth of masterpieces, the writer is fully confident of his techniques which, joined by a sufficient knowledge of the evolution of Chinese calligraphy and an aesthetic insight into the beauty of this abstract art, will touch off his urge to take a little adventure, and that adventure is rightly his freedom and hopefully, his unique style, a reward for all the patience and efforts he has invested over the years. By now at last, he is entitled to make all his own decisions on almost everything. I recall what an American professor from Tokyo University had said when he was learning Chinese calligraphy from me in Nanjing 29 years ago. He was quoting the Japanese who have a vivid description of leaning how to play the flute: "It takes one year to make a sound and three years to shake your head." The same is true of a pianist. When he is a beginner, he sits stiffly before the keyboard; when he becomes a master, his body can afford to rock most violently and his audience is stirred to frenzy and madness. And the same is true of Chinese calligraphy: It demands many years of disciplined practice, but is rewarded afterwards by a most free, poetic, and intoxicating instrument of self expression.

››› **Notes:**

1. Most scholars base their belief on the "Preface" to *Shuo Wen Jie Zi* (《说 文 解 字》), the first standard book on Chinese etymology, by Xu

Shen (许慎), a scholar in the Han Dynasty.

2. However, the *Yishan Bei* we see today is not the original one in Li Si's hand, but a copy made by Xu Xuan (徐铉) of the Southern Tang Dynasty.

3. The earliest relic of *mao bi* discovered so far dates back to the Warring States (475–221 B.C.), some 500 years prior to Han. q.v. *References on Cultural Relics* (《文物参考资料》), Vol. 12, 1954.

4. Also called *zhen shu* (真 书), the "genuine script," or *zheng shu* (正书), the "correct script."

5. *Twenty Pieces in Longmen* is a collective title given to the twenty inscriptions on the tombstones most characteristic of the calligraphic style of the Northern Wei period. Longmen is situated in Luoyang, Henan Province, most famous for its grottos, a treasure house of calligraphy, painted murals, and Buddhist sculptures.

6. Opinions differ as regards the order of learning the major scripts. While most teachers advise the *kai-xing-cao* sequence complemented by *li* and *zhuan*, some would argue for *zhuan* and *li* prior to all others, for the simple reason that *zhuan* and *li* are the very first two scripts created and all students of Chinese calligraphy are supposed to faithfully trace its historical trajectory.

7. The *cao shu* here only refers to *zhang cao—li shu* written in a quick and sketchy manner, and not *jin cao* or *kuang cao*, which are its later developments.

8. See Part One of *Shu Duan* (《书断・上》), Zhang's classification of the different calligraphic styles and schools up to his time and his judgment and ranking of all the renowned calligraphers since time immemorial.

9. For a detailed account of this fascinating story, see "Notes on the 'Record of the Orchard Pavilion Gathering' " (兰 亭 记) by He Yanzhi (何延之) of Tang in *Fa Shu Yao Lu* (《法书要录》), by Zhang Yanyuan (张彦远), a Tang calligraphic critic and historian. Beijing: People's Fines Arts Press, 1984. pp. 124–131.

10. Ebrey, Patricia Buckley. "Calligraphy as a Fine Art" in *China: Cambridge Illustrated History*. Cambridge: Cambridge University Press, 2004. p. 113.

11. De Mente, Boyé Lafayette. *The Chinese Have a Word for It: The Complete Guide to Chinese Thought and Culture*. Illinois: Passport Books, a division of NTC/Contemporary Publishing Group, Inc., 2000. pp. 359–360.

12. Chiang Yee is, if I guess aright, the same person as Chan Him in De Mente's book, for the quote below is almost exactly the same as the related part in Chiang's *Chinese Calligraphy: An Introduction to Its Aesthetic and Technique*.

13. De Mente, Boyé Lafayette. *The Chinese Have a Word for It: The Complete Guide to Chinese Thought and Culture*. p. 360.

14. Chiang Yee. *Chinese Calligraphy: An Introduction to Its Aesthetic and Technique*. Cambridge: Harvard University Press, 3rd edition, 1973. p. 110.

15. Reed, Herbert. "Preface" to Chiang's *Chinese Calligraphy*. p. Ⅶ.

16. Ibid., p. Ⅷ.
17. Madam Wei. "Bi Zhen Tu" ("笔阵图") in Zhang Yanyuan's *Fa Shu Yao Lu*. pp. 5–7.
18. Ibid., p.6. tr. Lin Yutang. *My Country and My People*. Beijing: Foreign Language Teaching and Research Press, 2004. p. 288.
19. Lin Yutang. *My Country and My People*. p. 285.
20. Ibid.
21. Ibid. p. 288.
22. Chiang Yee. *Chinese Calligraphy*. p. 126.
23. Ibid., p. 128.
24. Ibid., p. 129.
25. For a detailed discussion and analysis of the Wei calligraphy as against *kai shu* of Tang, see Bao Shichen's *Yi Zhou Shuang Ji* (《艺舟双楫》) and Kang Youwei's *Guang Yi Zhou Shuang Ji* (《广艺舟双楫》), an amplification and development of Bao's treatise, in *Selected Treatises on Calligraphy throughout the Ages* (《历代书法论文选》), compiled and collated by the Classics Studies Institute of Huadong Normal University. Shanghai: Calligraphy & Painting Press, 2000. pp. 640–679; pp. 747–868.
26. Lin Yutang. *My Country and My People*. p. 289.
27. There is no fixed requirement as to exactly how much time one should spend copying the models. Most would advise at least a couple of years for each of the five major script. In fact *lin tie* (临 帖), or imitating the copybooks, should be made a lifelong habit for anyone who prefers a calligraphic career.
28. While most scholars and artists emphasize the importance of moral character, some honestly believe that art has nothing to do with ethics. A case in point is Zhao Mengfu, who first served his Lord in the Song Dynasty, and when Song was exterminated and replaced by Yuan, became an official in the new imperial court, an act of betrayal, judging from the conventional cultural value of China, to his former master. But Zhao is universally recognized as one of the greatest calligraphers and painters in Chinese history. Therefore it might be more appropriate to say that art is closely related to one's character and not his moral character. In this respect, the notion is very similar to Buffon's celebrated dictum "*Le style, c'est l'homme même*" from his *Discours sur le style*.
29. Quoted from Lin Yutang. *My Country and My People*. p. 281.
30. *Xuan zhi* is named after Xuancheng (宣城), now renamed Xuanzhou (宣州), a town in Anhui Province, famed for its prosperous trading of the best-quality paper in China for both calligraphy and painting. But the place of its manufacture is not Xuancheng or Xuanzhou as most people mistakenly believe, but Jing County (泾县), also in Anhui. We don't know for sure when *xuan zhi* first came to artists' notice. But as far back as Tang at the least, it was already in wide use and extremely popular with the professionals. q.v. Zhang Yanyuan's *Notes on the Celebrated Paintings throughout the Ages* (《历代名画记》)
31. This part about the ink-slab is heavily based on Chiang Yee's Chinese Calligraphy. p. 136.

32. *Yong* (永) means "eternal" in Chinese. In the actual writing of Chinese characters, there are a lot more strokes than the eight in *yong*, although these eight are considered the most essential ones.
33. Quoted in Chiang Yee's *Chinese Calligraphy*. p. 200.
34. I am in deep debt to Mr Chiang Yee for the introduction of the "three stages." See Chiang's *Chinese Calligraphy*. p. 196.

Introduction to Laozi and His *Daodejing*

Bill Porter

The *Daodejing* (道德经) is at heart a simple book. Written at the end of the sixth century BC by a man called Laozi (老子), it is a vision of what our lives would be like if we were more like the dark, new moon.

Bill Porter

Laozi teaches us that the dark can always become light and contains within itself the potential for growth and long life, while the light can only become dark and brings with it decay and early death. Laozi chose long life. Thus he chose the dark.

The word that Laozi chose to represent this vision was *Dao* (道). But *Dao* means "road" or "way" and doesn't appear to have anything to do with darkness. The character is made up of two graphs: "首: head" and "辶: go." To make sense of how the character came to be constructed, early Chinese philologists concluded that "head" must mean the start of something and that the two graphs together show someone starting on a trip. But a Chinese scholar in Taiwan has recently presented a novel, and more convincing interpretation of the word's origins. According to Du Erwei (杜而未), the "head" in the character *dao* is the face of the moon. And the meaning of "road" comes from watching this disembodied face as it moves across the sky.

Du also notes that *dao* shares a common linguistic heritage with words that mean "moon" in other cultures: Tibetans call the moon *da-ua;* the Miao, who now live in southwest China but who lived in the same state as Laozi when he was alive, call it *Dao-tie;* the ancient Egyptians called it *thoth.* Du Erwei could have also added *dar-sha,* which means "new moon" in Sanskrit.

However, the heart of Du's thesis is not linguistic, but textual and based on references within the *Daodejing.* Laozi says the Dao is between Heaven and Earth, it's Heaven's Gate, it's empty but inexhaustible, it doesn't die, it waxes and wanes, it's distant and dark, it doesn't try to be full, it's the light that doesn't blind, it has thirty spokes and two thirteen-day (visible) phases, it can be strung like a bow or expand and contract like a bellows, it moves the other way (in relation to the sun), it's the great image, the hidden immortal, the crescent soul, the dark union, the dark womb, the dark beyond dark. If this isn't the moon, what is it?

Du Erwei has, I think, uncovered a deep and primitive layer of the *Daodejing* that has escaped the attention of other scholars. Of course, we cannot say for certain that Laozi was consciously aware of the Dao's association with the moon. But we have his images, and they are too often lunar to dismiss as accidental.

In associating the Dao with the moon, Laozi was not alone. The symbol Taoists have used since ancient times to represent the Dao ☯ shows the two conjoined phases of the moon. And how could they ignore such an obvious connection between its cycle of change and our own? Every month we watch the moon grow from nothing to a luminous disc that scatters the stars and pulls the tides within us all. The oceans feel it. The earth feels it. Plants and animals feel it. Humans also feel it, though it is women who seem to be most aware of it. In the *Huangdi Neijing* (黄帝内经), or *Yellow Emperor's Internal Book of Medicine*, Qi Bo (岐伯) explained to the Yellow Emperor: "When the moon begins to grow, blood and breath begin to surge. When the moon is completely full, blood and breath are at their fullest, tendons and muscles are at their strongest. When the moon is completely empty, tendons and muscles are at their weakest."

The advance of civilization has separated us from this easy lunar awareness. We call people affected by the moon "lunatics," making clear our disdain for its power. Laozi redirects our vision to this ancient mirror. But instead of pointing to its light, he points to its darkness. Every month the moon effortlessly shows us that something comes from nothing. Laozi asks us to emulate this aspect of the moon, not the full moon, which is destined to wane, but the new moon, which holds the promise of rebirth. And while he has us gazing at the moon's dark mirror, he asks why we don't live longer than we do. After all, don't we share the same nature as the moon, and isn't the moon immortal?

Scholars tend to ignore Laozi's emphasis on darkness and immortality, for it takes the book beyond the reach of academic analysis. For them, darkness is just a more poetic way of describing the mysterious. And immortality is a euphemism for long life. Over the years, they have distilled what they call Laozi's "Taoist philosophy" from the later developments of "Taoist religion." They call the *Daodejing* a treatise on political or military strategy, or they see it as primitive scientific naturalism or utopianism—or just a bunch of sayings.

But trying to force the *Daodejing* into the categories of modern discourse not only distorts the *Daodejing*, it also treats the traditions that later Taoists have associated with the text as irrelevant and misguided.

Meanwhile, the *Daodejing* continues to inspire millions of Chinese as a spiritual text, and I have tried to present it in that dark light. The words of philosophers fail here. If words are of any use at all, they are the words of the poet. For poetry has the ability to point us toward the truth and then stand aside, while prose stands in the doorway relating all the wonders on the other side but rarely lets us pass.

In this respect, the *Daodejing* is unique among the great literary works of the Zhou dynasty. Aside from the anonymous poems and folksongs of the *Shijing* (诗经), or *Book of Odes*, we have no other poetic work from this early period of Chinese history; the wisdom of other sages was conveyed in prose. Although I haven't attempted to reproduce Laozi's poetic devices [Xu Yongzhang (许永璋) identifies twenty-eight different kinds of rhyme], I have tried to convey the poetic feel with which he strings together images for our breath and spirit, but not necessarily our minds. For the *Daodejing* is one long poem written in praise of something we cannot name, much less imagine.

Despite the elusiveness and namelessness of the Dao, Laozi tells us we can approach it through *De* (德). *De* means "virtue," both in the sense of "moral character" as well as "power to act." Yan Lingfeng (严灵峰) says, "Virtue is the manifestation of the Way. The Way is what Virtue contains. Without the Way, Virtue would have no power. Without Virtue, the Way would have no appearance" (*Daodejing*, 21). Han Fei (韩非) put it more simply: "*De* is the Dao at work" (*Daodejing*, 38). *De* is our entrance to the Dao. *De* is what we cultivate. Laozi's Virtue, however, isn't the virtue of adhering to a moral code but action that involves no moral code, no self, no other—no action.

These are the two poles around which the *Daodejing* turns: the Dao, the dark, the body, the essence, the Way; and *De*, the light, the function, the spirit, the Virtue. In terms of origin, the Dao comes first. In terms of practice, *De* comes first. The dark gives the light a place to shine. The light allows us to see the dark. But too much light blinds. Laozi saw everyone chasing the light and hastening their own destruction. He encouraged people to choose the dark instead of the light, less instead of more, weakness instead of strength, inaction instead of action. What could be simpler?

Laozi's preference for darkness extended to himself as well. For the past 2,500 years, the Chinese have revered the *Daodejing* as they have no other book, and yet they know next to nothing about its author. What they do know, or think they know, is contained in a brief biographical sketch included by Sima Qian (司马迁) in a history of ancient China that he completed around 100 BC. Although we don't know what Sima Qian's sources of information were, we do know he was considered the most widely travelled man of his age, and he went to great lengths to verify the information he used. Of late it has become popular, if not *de rigueur*, to debunk his account of Laozi, but it remains the earliest account we have and is worth repeating.

According to Sima Qian, Laozi was a native of Huxian Prefecture (苦县) in the state of Chu (楚). Nowadays, the former prefectural town of Huxian is called Luyi (鹿邑). If you are travelling in China, or simply want to find it on a map, look for the town of Shangqiu (商丘) on the train line that runs between the city of Zhengzhou (郑州) on the Yellow River and the Grand Canal town of Xuzhou (徐州). Luyi is about 70 kilometers south of Shangqiu. The shrine that marks the site of Laozi's former village is just east of town.

The region is known as the Huanghuai Plain (黄淮平原). As its name suggests, it is the result of the regular flooding of the Huanghe, or Yellow River, to the north and the Huaihe, or Huai River, to the south. The Chinese have been growing wheat and millet here since neolithic times, and more recently cotton and tobacco. It remains one of the most productive agricultural areas in all of China, and it was a rich prize over which many states fought in ancient times.

Laozi was born on this plain in 604 BC, or 571 BC, depending on which account of later historians we accept. Sima Qian doesn't give us a date, but he does say that Huxian was part of the great state of Chu. Officially, Huxian belonged to the small state of Chen (陈) until 479 BC, when Chu eliminated Chen as a state once and for all. Some scholars have interpreted this to mean that either Huxian did not belong to Chu when Laozi was alive or that he must have been born there after 479 BC. But we need not accept either conclusion. Sima Qian would have been aware that Chu controlled the fortunes of Chen as early as 598 BC, when Chu briefly annexed

Taiqinggong Village (太清宫村) east of Huxian. Laozi's old home was located on this, the fifth of nine bends of a canal that once enabled small boats to travel via adjoining waterways to the Yellow River to the north or the Huai River to the south.

the entire state and then changed its mind, allowing Chen to exist as a "neighbor state."

Whether or not Huxian was actually part of Chu is not important. What is important is that during the sixth century BC Chu controlled the region of which Huxian was a part. This is significant not for verifying the accuracy of Sima Qian's account but for directing our attention to the cultural influence that Chu represented. Chu was not like the other states in the central plains.

Although the rulers of Chu traced their ancestry to a grandson of the Yellow Emperor, the patriarch of Chinese culture, they represented its shamanistic periphery. From their ancestral home in the Songshan (嵩山) area, just south of the Yellow River, they moved, or were pushed, steadily southwest, eventually ending up in the Jingshan (荆山) area, just north of the Yangtze. Over the centuries, they mixed with other tribal groups, such as the Miao, and incorporated elements of their shamanistic cultures. The Chu rulers took for their surname the word *xiong* (熊), meaning "bear," and they called themselves Man (蛮) or Yi (夷), which the Chinese in the central states interpreted to mean "barbarians."

The influence of Chu's culture on Laozi is impossible to determine, but it does help us better understand the *Daodejing* knowing that it was written by a man who was no stranger to shamanistic conceptions of the sacred world. Certainly as Daoism developed in later centuries, it remained heavily indebted to shamanism, and some scholars see evidence of the Chu dialect in the *Daodejing* itself.

This, then, was the region where Laozi grew up. But his name was not Laozi (which means "Old Master"). Sima Qian says his family name was Li (李), his personal name was Er (耳) (meaning "ear," and hence, learned), and his posthumous name was Dan (聃) (meaning "long-eared," and hence, wise). In addition to providing us with a complete set of names, Sima Qian also tells us that Laozi, or Li Er, served as Keeper of the Royal Archives.

Before continuing, I should note that some scholars reject Sima Qian's Li Er or Li Dan and suggest instead a man named Lao Dan (老聃), who also served as Keeper of the Royal Archives, but in the fourth century BC rather than the sixth century. Some find this later date more acceptable in explaining Laozi's innovative literary style as well as in explaining why Zhuangzi (庄子) attributes passages of the *Daodejing* to Lao Dan but not Li Dan. For his part, Sima Qian was certainly familiar with Zhuangzi's writings, and he was not unaware of the fourth-century historian Lao Dan. In fact, he admits that some people thought that Lao Dan was Laozi. But Sima Qian was not convinced that the two were the same man. After all, if Dan was Laozi's posthumous name, why shouldn't Zhuangzi and other later writers call him "Old Dan" ? And why couldn't there be two record keepers with the same name in the course of two centuries? If China's Grand Historian was not convinced that the fourth-century historian was the author of the *Daodejing*—certainly he had more documents at his disposal than we now possess—I see no reason to decide in favor of a man whose only claim to fame was to prophesize the ascendency of the state of Qin (秦), which was to bring the Zhou dynasty to an end in 221 BC. Meanwhile, I think I hear Laozi laughing.

In any case, the place where Laozi kept the archives was the Zhou dynasty capital of Luoyang (洛 阳), which was about 300 kilometers west of Huxian. Luoyang was a neolithic campsite as early as 3000 BC and a military garrison during the first dynasties: the Xia (夏) and Shang (商). When the state of Zhou overthrew the Shang dynasty in 1122 BC, the Duke of Zhou built a new subsidiary capital around the old garrison. He dubbed it *Wangcheng* (王城): City of the King. Usually, though, the king lived in one of the new dynasty's two western capitals of Feng (丰) and Hao (镐), near modern Xi'an (西安). But when these were destroyed in 771 BC, Wangcheng became the sole royal residence. And this is where Laozi spent his time recording the events at court.

Laozi must have been busy in the years following the death of King Jing (周景王). When King Jing died in 520 BC, two of his sons, Prince Chao (朝) and Prince Jing (敬), both declared themselves his successor. At first Prince Chao gained the upper hand, and Prince Jing was forced to leave the capital. But with the help of other nobles, Prince Jing soon returned and established another capital fifteen kilometers to the east of Wangcheng, which he dubbed *Chengzhou* (成 周): Glory of Zhou. And in 516 BC, Prince Jing finally succeeded in driving his brother from the old capital.

In the same year, the Keeper of the Royal Archives, which were still in Wangcheng, received a visitor from the state of Lu (鲁). The visitor was a young man named Kong Fuzi (孔夫子), or Confucius. Confucius was interested in ritual and asked Laozi about the ceremonies of the ancient kings.

According to Sima Qian, Laozi responded with this advice: "The ancients you admire have been in the ground a long time. Their bones have turned to dust. Only their words remain. Those among them who were wise rode in carriages when times were good and slipped quietly away when times were bad. I have heard that the clever merchant hides his wealth so his store looks empty and that the superior man acts dumb so he can avoid calling attention to himself. I advise you to get rid of your excessive pride and ambition. They won't do you any good. This is all I have to say to you." Afterwards, Confucius told his disciples, "Today when I met Laozi, it was like meeting a dragon."

The story of this meeting appears in a sufficient number of ancient texts to make it unlikely that it was invented by Taoists. Confucian records also report it taking place. According to the traditional account, Laozi was eighty-eight years old when he met Confucius. If so, and if he was born in 604 BC, the two sages would have met in 516 BC, and Confucius would have been thirty-five. So it is possible, though Confucius would not have had many disciples at such an early date.

Following his meeting with Confucius, Laozi decided to take his own advice, and he left the capital by ox-cart. And he had good reason to leave. For when Prince Chao was banished from Wangcheng, he took with him the royal archives, the same archives of which Laozi was supposedly in charge. If Laozi needed a reason to leave, he certainly had one in 516 BC.

With the loss of the archives, Laozi was out of a job. He was also, no doubt, fed up with the prospects for enlightened rule in the Middle Kingdom. Hence, he headed not for his hometown of Huxian to the east but for Hangu Pass (函谷关), which was 150 kilometers west of Luoyang, and which served as the border between the Zhou dynasty's central states and the semi-barbarian state of Qin, which now controlled the area surrounding the dynasty's former western capitals.

As Keeper of the Royal Archives, Laozi no doubt supplied himself with the necessary documents to get through what was the most strategic pass in all of China. Hardly wide enough for two carts, it forms a seventeen-kilometer-long defile through a plateau of loess that has blown down from the north

Hangu Pass. Midway between the Zhou dynasty's eastern and western capitals and situated between the Yellow River and the Zhongnan Mountains. This is where Laozi met Yin Xi, Warden of the Pass.

and accumulated between the Zhongnan Mountains (终南山) and the Yellow River over the past million years. In ancient times, the Chinese said that whoever controlled Hangu Pass controlled China. It was so easy to defend that during the Second World War the Japanese army failed to break through it, despite finding no difficulty in sweeping Chinese forces from the plains to the east.

Fortunately, Laozi was expected. According to Taoist records, Master Yin Xi (尹喜) was studying the heavens far to the west at the royal observatory at Louguantai (楼观台), when he noticed a purple vapor drifting from the east. He deduced that a sage would soon be passing through the area, and he knew that anyone travelling west would have to come through Hangu Pass. Hence he proceeded to the pass.

Sima Qian, however, says Yin Xi was Warden of the Pass and makes no mention of his association with Louguantai. When Laozi appeared, Yin Xi recognized the sage and asked for instruction. According to Sima Qian, Laozi gave Yin Xi the *Daodejing* and then continued on to distant, unknown realms.

Taoists agree that Laozi continued on from Hangu

Louguantai. The small knoll beyond the gravel bed of the Tianyu River (田峪河) *and at the foot of the Zhongnan Mountains is where Taoists say Laozi wrote the* Daodejing.

Pass, but in the company of Yin Xi, who invited him to his observatory 250 kilometers to the west. Taoists say Laozi stopped long enough at Louguantai to convey the teachings that make up his *Daodejing* and then travelled on through Sanguan Pass (大散关), another 150 kilometers to the west, and into the state of Shu (蜀). Shu was founded by a branch of the same lineage that founded the state of Chu, although its rulers revered the cuckoo rather than the bear. And in the land of the cuckoo, Laozi finally achieved anonymity as well as immortality.

Curiously, about six kilometers west of Louguantai, there's a tombstone with Laozi's name on it. The Red Guards knocked it down in the 1960s, and when I last visited Louguantai in 1993 it was still down. I asked Louguantai's abbot, Ren Farong (任法融), what happened to Laozi. Did he continue on through Sanguan Pass, or was he buried at Louguantai? Master Ren suggested both stories were true. As Confucius noted, Laozi was a dragon among men. And being a member of the serpent family, why should we wonder at his ability to leave his skin behind and continue on through cloud-barred passes?

And so, Laozi, whoever he was and whenever he lived, disappeared and left behind his small book. The book at first didn't have a name. When writers like Mozi (墨子) and Wenzi (文子) quoted from it in the fifth century BC, or Zhuangzi and Liezi (列子) quoted from it in the fourth century BC, or Han Fei explained passages in the third century BC and Huainanzi (淮南子) in the second century BC, they simply said "Laozi says this" or "Lao Dan says that." And so people started calling the source of all these quotes from *Laozi.*

Sima Qian also mentioned no name. He only said that Laozi wrote a book, and it was divided into two parts. About the same time, people started calling these two parts *The Way* and *Virtue*, after the first lines of verses 1 and 38. And to these, were added the honorific *jing* (经), meaning "ancient text." And so Laozi's book was called the *Daodejing*, the *Book of Dao and De*.

In addition to its two parts, it was also divided into separate verses. But, as with other ancient texts, punctuation and enumeration of passages were left up to the reader. About the same time that Sima Qian wrote his biography of Laozi and people started calling the book the *Daodejing*, Yan Zun (严遵) produced a commentary in the first century BC that divided the text into seventy-two verses. A century earlier, or a couple of centuries later, no one knows which, He Shanggong (河上公) divided the same basic text into eighty-one verses. And a thousand years later, Wu Cheng (吴澄) tried a sixty-eight-verse division. But the system that has persisted through the centuries is that of He Shanggong, who also gave each verse its own title.

The text itself has seen dozens of editions containing anywhere from five to six thousand characters. The numerical discrepancy is not as significant as it might appear and is largely the result of adding certain grammatical particles for clarity or omitting them for brevity. The greatest difference among editions centers not on the number of characters but on the rendering of certain phrases and the presence or absence of certain lines.

Over the centuries, several emperors have taken it upon themselves to resolve disputes concerning the choice among these variants. And the creation of a standard edition has resulted from their efforts. The standard edition, however, is still open to revision, and every student of the *Daodejing* repeats the process of choosing among variants to understand the text.

In this regard, *Daodejing* studies were blessed in late 1973 with the discovery of two copies of the text in a tomb that was sealed in 168 BC in a suburb of the provincial capital of Changsha (长沙) known as Mawangdui (马王堆). Despite the lapse of over 2,100 years, the copies, written on silk, were in remarkably good condition.

Gao Zhixi (高志喜), who supervised their removal and who directed the Mawangdui

Museum until just recently, attributes their preservation to layers of clay and charcoal that covered the tomb. At least this is his official explanation. In private, he says their preservation could have also been due to the presence of an unknown gas created by the decomposition of certain substances inside the tomb. He tried to take a sample of the gas, but the discovery was made in the middle of the Cultural Revolution, and he spent two days peddling his bicycle around Changsha before he found anyone who would loan him the necessary equipment. By then the gas was gone.

The books, though, made up for his disappointment. Along with the *Daodejing* there were several hitherto unknown commentaries on the *Yijing* (易经) as well as a number of lost texts attributed to the Yellow Emperor. The Chinese Academy of Sciences immediately convened a committee of scholars to examine these texts and decipher illegible sections.

In the years since their discovery, the two Mawangdui copies of the *Daodejing* have contributed greatly to the elucidation of a number of difficult and previously misunderstood passages. Without them, I would have been forced to choose among unsatisfactory variants on too many occasions. Still, the Mawangdui texts contain numerous omissions and errors and need to be used with great care.

Fortunately, we also have another text that dates from the same period. Like the Mawangdui texts, it was discovered in a tomb that was sealed shortly after 200 BC. This tomb was located near the Grand Canal town of Xuzhou and was opened in 574 AD. Not long afterward, the court astrologer Fu Yi (傅奕) published an edition of the copy of the *Daodejing* that was found inside.

In addition to the Mawangdui and Fuyi texts, we also have more than sixty copies of the text that were found shortly after 1900 in the Silk Road oasis of Dunhuang (敦煌). Most of these copies date from the eighth and ninth centuries. However, one of them was written by a man named Suo Dan (索 紞) in 270 AD, giving us yet another early hand-written edition to consider.

We also have a copy of the *Daodejing* written by the great fourth-century calligrapher Wang Xizhi (王羲之), as well as a dozen or so stelae on which various emperors had the entire text carved. Finally, we have the text as it appears in such early commentaries as those of Yan Zun, He Shanggong, and Wang Bi (王弼) (not to mention numerous passages quoted in the ancient works of Mozi, Wenzi, Zhuangzi, Liezi, Han Fei, Huainanzi, and others).

In undertaking this translation, I have consulted nearly all of these editions and have produced a new recension incorporating my choices among the readings. For the benefit of those able to read Chinese, I have included the resulting text with my translation. I have also added a number of commentaries.

Over the centuries, some of China's greatest writers have devoted themselves to explaining the *Daodejing*, and no Chinese would think of reading the text without the help of at least one of these line-by-line or verse-by-verse explanations. When I first decided to translate the *Daodejing*, it occurred to me that Western readers are at a serious disadvantage without the help of such materials. To remedy this situation, I have collected several dozen of the better-known commentaries along with a few that are more obscure, and I have selected from among them those passages that provide important background information or insights.

I have also added a few remarks of my own, though I have usually limited these to textual issues. In this regard, I have tried to restrict myself to those lines where my choice among variants may have resulted in a significant departure from other translations that readers might have in their possession. The *Daodejing* is, after all, one of the most translated books in the world, exceeded only by the *Bible* and the *Bhagavad-Gita*.

Since the text first appeared in Latin in 1788, more than a hundred translations have been published in the English language alone, and readers could not be blamed for wondering if there isn't something inherent in the text that infects those who read it with the desire to produce even more translations.

My own attempt to add to this number dates back nearly twenty-five years to when I attended a course in Taiwan given by John C. H. Wu (吴经熊). Professor Wu had himself produced an excellent English translation of the *Daodejing*, and he offered a course on the subject to graduate students in the philosophy department at the College of Chinese Culture, which I was attending between stays at Buddhist temples.

Once a week, about six of us filed past the guards at the stately Zhongshanlou (中山 楼) on Yangmingshan (阳明 山), where the government had provided Professor Wu with a bungalow in recognition of his long service. In addition to translating the *Daodejing*, Professor Wu also translated the *New Testament*. Once a week, we nipped tea, ate his wife's cookies, and discussed a verse or two of Laozi's text. Between classes, I tried translating the odd line in the margins of Professor Wu's bilingual edition, but I did not get far. After one semester, the course ended, and I moved to a Buddhist monastery in the hills south of Taipei, where I put aside Laozi's text in favor of Buddhist sutras and poetry. But ever since then, I have been waiting for an opportunity to dust off this thinnest of ancient books and resume my earlier attempt at translation.

The opportunity finally presented itself when I recently returned to America after more than twenty years in Taiwan and Hong Kong. In the early seventies, when I was attending graduate school at Columbia University, I recall Professor Bielenstein quoting W. A. C. H. Dobson, who said it was time for a Sinologist to retire when he announced he was working on a new translation of the *Daodejing*. And so I have joined the ranks of the retired.

I don't know if Dobson would have approved. His remarks, I suspect, were intended more as friendly criticism of the presumption that translating the *Daodejing* entails. Though relatively brief, the *Daodejing* is a difficult text. But it is also a transparent one.

For the past two years, one image that has repeatedly come to mind while working on this translation is skating on a newly frozen lake near my home in Idaho when I was a boy. Sometimes the ice was so clear, I felt like I was skating across the night sky, and the only sounds I could hear were the cracks that echoed through the dark, transparent depths. I thought if the ice ever gave way I would find myself on the other side of the universe, and I always carried ice picks just in case I had to pull myself out. The ice never broke. But I've been hearing those cracks again.

Selections from *Daodejing*

Translated by Bill Porter

1

道可道。非恒道。名可名。非恒名。無名天地之始。有名萬物之母。故恒無欲以觀其妙。恒有欲以觀其徼。此兩者同。出而異名。同謂之玄。玄之又玄。眾妙之門。

The way that becomes a way
is not the Immortal Way
the name that becomes a name
is not the Immortal Name
the maiden of Heaven and Earth
has no name
the mother of all things has a
name
thus in innocence we see the
beginning
in passion we see the end
two different names
for one and the same
the one we call dark
the dark beyond dark
the door to all beginnings

8

上善若水。水善利萬物。而不爭。處眾人之所惡。故幾於道。居善地。心善淵。與善仁。言善信。政善治。事善能。動善時。夫唯不爭。故無尤。

The best are like water
bringing help to all
without competing
choosing what others avoid
hence approaching the Tao
dwelling with earth
thinking with depth
helping with kindness
speaking with truth
governing with peace
working with skill
moving with time
and because they don't compete
they aren't maligned

9

持而盈之。不如其已。揣而銳之。不可長保。金玉盈室。莫之能守。富貴而驕。自遺其咎。功遂身退。天之道也。

Instead of pouring in more
better stop while you can
making it sharper
won't help it last longer
houses full of treasure
can never be safe
the vanity of success
invites its own failure
retire when your work is done
this is the Way of Heaven

12

五色使人目盲。五音使人耳聾。五味使人口爽。馳騁畋獵使人心發狂。難得之貨使人行妨。是以聖人之治。為腹而不為目。故去彼而取此。

The five colors make our eyes blind
the five tones make our ears deaf
the five flavors make our mouths numb
riding and hunting make our minds wild
hard-to-get goods make us break laws
thus the rule of the sage
puts the stomach ahead of the eyes
thus he picks this over that

18

大道廢。安有仁義。智慧出。安有大偽。六親不和。安有孝慈。邦家昏亂。安有貞臣。

When the Great Way disappears
we meet kindness and justice
when reason appears
we meet great deceit
when the six relations fail
we meet obedience and love
when the country is in chaos
we meet honest officials

22

曲則全。枉則正。窪則盈。弊則新。少則得。多則惑。是以聖人執一。以為天下牧。不自視故明。不自見故章。不自伐故有功。不自矜故能長。夫唯不爭。故莫能與之爭。古之所謂曲則全者。幾語哉。成全而之。

Partial means whole
crooked means straight
hollow means full
worn-out means new
less means content
more means confused
thus the sage holds onto the one
to use in guiding the world
not watching himself he appears
not displaying himself he flourishes
not flattering himself he succeeds
not parading himself he leads
because he doesn't compete
no one can compete against him
the ancients who said partial
means whole
came close indeed
becoming whole depends on this

25

有物混成。先天地生。肅兮寥兮。獨立而不改。周行而不殆。可以為天下母。吾不知其名。字之曰道。吾強為之。名曰大。大曰逝。逝曰遠。遠曰反。故大。天大。地大。王亦大。國中有四大。而王居一焉。人法地。地法天。天法道。道法自然。

Imagine a nebulous thing
here before Heaven and Earth
silent and elusive
it stands alone not wavering
it travels everywhere unharmed
it could be the mother of us all
not knowing its name
I call it the Tao
forced to name it
I name it Great
great means ever-flowing
ever-flowing means far-reaching
far-reaching means returning
the Tao is great
Heaven is great
Earth is great
the king is also great
the realm contains four greats
of these the king is one
Man imitates Earth
Earth imitates Heaven
Heaven imitates the Tao
the Tao imitates itself

33

知人者智。自知者明。勝人者有力。自勝者強。知足者富。強行者有志。不失其所者久。死而不亡者壽。

Who knows others is perceptive
who knows himself is wise
who conquers others is forceful
who conquers himself is strong
who knows contentment is wealthy
who strives hard succeeds
who doesn't lose his place endures
who dies but doesn't perish lives on

36

將欲歙之。必固張之。將欲弱之。必固強之。將欲廢之。必固興之。將欲取之。必固予之。是謂微明。柔弱勝強。魚不可脫於淵。國之利器。不可以示人。

What you would shorten
you should therefore lengthen
what you would weaken
you should therefore strengthen
what you would topple
you should therefore raise
what you would take
you should therefore give
this is called hiding the light
the weak conquering the strong
fish can't survive out of the deep
a state's greatest tool
is not meant to be shown

41

上士聞道。勤而行之。中士聞道。若存若亡。下士聞道。大笑之。不笑不足以為道。是以建言有之曰。明道若昧。
進道若退。夷道若類。上德若穀。大白若辱。廣德不足。建德若偷。質真若渝。大方無隅。大器免成。大音希聲。大
象無形。道隱無名。夫唯道。善始且善成。

When a great person hears of the Way
he follows it with devotion
when an average person hears of the Way
he doesn't know if it's real or not
when a small person hears of the Way
he laughs out loud
if he didn't laugh
it wouldn't be the Way
hence these sayings arose
the brightest path seems dark
the quickest path seems slow
the smoothest path seems rough
the highest virtue low
the whitest white pitch-black
the greatest virtue wanting
the staunchest virtue timid
the truest truth uncertain
the perfect square lacks corners
the perfect tool does nothing
the perfect sound is hushed
the perfect form is shapeless
the Tao is hidden and has no name
but because it's the Tao
it knows how to start and how to finish

44

名與身。孰親。身與貨。孰多。得與亡。孰病。甚愛。必大費。多藏。必厚亡。知足。不辱。知止。不殆。可以長久。

Which is more vital
fame or health
which is more precious
health or riches
which is more harmful
loss or gain
the deeper the love
the higher the cost
the bigger the treasure
the greater the loss
who knows contentment
suffers no shame
who knows restraint
encounters no trouble
and thus lives long

46

天下有道。卻走馬以糞。天下無道。戎馬生於郊。罪莫大於可欲。禍莫大於不知足。咎莫憯於欲得。故知足之。恒足矣。

When the Tao prevails
courier horses manure fields
instead of roads
when the Tao fails
war-horses are raised on the
border
no crime is worse than yielding
to desire
no wrong is greater than
discontent
no curse is crueler than getting
what you want
the contentment of being content
is true contentment indeed

63

為無為。事無事。味無味。大小多少。報怨以德。圖難於其易。為大於其細。天下之難作于易。天下之大作於細。是以聖人終不為大。故能成其大。夫輕諾必寡信。多易必多難。是以聖人猶難之。故終於無難。

Act without acting
work without working
taste without tasting
great or small many or few
repay each wrong with virtue
plan for the hard while it's easy
work on the great while it's
small
the hardest task in the world
begins easy
the greatest goal in the world
begins small
therefore the sage never acts
great
he thus achieves great things
who quickly agrees is seldom
trusted
who makes it all easy finds it all
hard
therefore the sage makes everything
hard
he thus finds nothing hard

64

其安易持。其未兆易謀。其脆易破。其微易散。為之於未有。治之於未亂。合抱之木生於毫末。九層之台起於累土。千里之行始於足下。為之者敗之。執之者失之。是以聖人無為。故無敗。無執。故無失。民之從事。恒于幾成而敗之。慎終如始。則無敗事矣。是以聖人欲不欲。而不貴難得之貨。學不學。而複眾人之所過。以輔萬物之自然。而不敢為。

It's easy to rule while it's peaceful
it's easy to plan before it arrives
it's easy to break while it's fragile
it's easy to disperse while it's small
act before it exists
govern before it rebels
a giant tree grows from the tiniest shoot
a great tower rises from a basket of dirt
a thousand-mile journey begins at your feet
but to act is to fail
to control is to lose
therefore the sage doesn't act
he thus doesn't fail
he doesn't control
he thus doesn't lose
when people pursue a task
they always fail near the end
care at the end as well as the start
means an end to failure
the sage thus seeks what no one seeks
he doesn't prize hard-to-get goods
he studies what no one studies
he turns to what others pass by
to help all things be natural
he thus dares not act

80

小國寡民。使有十百人之器。而不用。使民重死。而不遠徙。有舟輿。無所乘之。有甲兵。無所陳之。使人複結繩而用之。甘其食。美其服。安其居。樂其俗。鄰邦相望。雞犬之聲相聞。民至老死。不相往來。

Imagine a small state with a
small population
let there be labor-saving tools
that aren't used
let people consider death
and not move far
let there be boats and carts
but no reason to ride them
let there be armor and weapons
but no reason to employ them
let people return to the use of
knots
and be satisfied with their food
and pleased with their clothing
and content with their homes
and happy with their customs
let there be a state so near
people hear its dogs and chickens
and live out their lives
without making a visit

81

True words aren't beautiful
beautiful words aren't true
the good aren't eloquent
the eloquent aren't good
the wise aren't learned
the learned aren't wise
the sage accumulates nothing
but the more he does for others
the greater his existence
the more he gives to others
the greater his abundance
the Way of Heaven
is to help without harming
the Way of the sage
is to act without struggling

信言不美。美言不信。善者不辯。辯者不善。知者不博。博者不知。聖人不積。既以為人。己愈有。既以與人。己愈多。天之道。利而不害。聖人之道。為而不爭。

Short Stories

Wealth, Blessings and Longevity

Pang Yu / 庞　羽
Translated by Denis Mair

Some books he had heaped on the floor were gone, because Maddy Yuan had thrown them away. "Why did you throw them out?" Hua Yuqing asked her. Without saying a word, Maddy Yuan threw two magazines in the trash bin, right in front of him, then returned to the kitchen to chop vegetables. Hua Yuqing was still asking questions when—*thok*—she forcefully brought the knife blade down on the chopping block, causing Hua's neck to shrink down between his shoulders. Maddy Yuan wrapped a cloth around her hand: "Lift your arm." Hua obediently raised his arm. "Turn around." Hua turned docilely. Maddy Yuan rubbed the cloth over his upper body, and then buffed his shoes until they shone. "Alright now, go off to play cards with Old Zhang." Hua Yuqing's grim-set features darkened as he spun about and propelled his wheelchair toward the apartment door. At the door he held back his wheels for a moment, but Maddy Yuan shot him a look. "Get moving." Being a second-level professor[1] from Southtomb University made no difference: he did as he was told. On the way out, he leaned his head back into the room: "Make fish and noodle soup, and two eggs. You got that? Two eggs!"

Old Zhang was not much of a cardplayer, but Hua Yuqing didn't mind. Other codgers in the housing complex had nasty habits like spitting up phlegm or picking their noses, but Old Zhang did not. Old Zhang would elegantly pull out a piece of tissue and turn his head aside, not letting people see what he was up to. There were other points that raised Old Zhang in Hua's estimation, especially Zhang's habit of washing his hands before sitting down to the card table. The sound of water tinkling in the sink gave Hua a bracing feeling, like a jolt of electricity.

Since his lower-body paralysis had set in, Hua Yuqing rarely went out the gate. At age 28 he had been fast-tracked into a professorship; at 34 he had won the "Guo Moruo Gold Cup" National Award in the Humanities and Social Sciences; at 40 he got tenure at Southtomb University. After such an impressive string of victories, he was weary of the academic battlefield.

One day he sat in his bedroom, gazing upon the trophies he had won over the years. Having gazed to a point of deep abstraction, he shouted for Maddy Yuan. She came running in her apron, muttering under her breath, and asked what had gotten into him. Big tears were running down his face. He didn't want to die this way; he wanted to go outside.

Maddy Yuan's original name was Tian Enyuan, and she used to live in Maville. She was married to Ma Dongqiang, and they had brought up two sons and one daughter. Her oldest son was a migrant worker in Shenzhen; her second son was jobless and lived at home. Her daughter, who had come along to the city, was named Orchid Ma; she had a square face with gooseberry eyes, wide ears and a heifer-like nose. Her arms and legs were well-formed. Orchid liked to say outrageous things to people. The first thing out of her mouth might dismay them, and the second usually left them speechless. Maddy Yuan did not try to curb Orchid's impulsive tongue. You could never tell—some young fool might find it charming.

The move from Maville to Pei City had been a well-calculated scheme for Maddy Yuan. Take for instance the one-room flat at #18 Tongriver Road. Maddy Yuan had checked the place out again and again; she had bargained over room rates, until finally she found herself this temporary dwelling. Take for instance her Aima electric scooter: she had bitten the bullet for the purchase. Going out to buy groceries or taking care of errands, she couldn't get along without a conveyance. Take for example her eldest son: he was earning money, so he could look for a wife on his own. As for her second son, he was a good-for-nothing, so just let him be. As for Orchid Ma, if only she found herself a young man in the city, her life would be better than her mother's. And finally she succeeded in insinuating herself into the Hua household, infiltrating the world of intellectuals.

Hua Yuqing had originally resisted Maddy Yuan, finding her coarse and inelegant. Later he discovered a certain delicacy within that coarseness. The only drawback was, she was a bit too free with curses, as if her mouth had been lubricated to let coarse language slip out. Yet this was not the main consideration. Hua Yuqing had known success in his career, but his legs were paralyzed. His wife was gone, and his son was in America. No matter how much he paid, there weren't many people who'd be willing to wait on him, an invalid, hand and foot. What is more, Hua Yuqing liked to eat fish, all kinds of fish. Maddy Yuan's fish and noodle soup was unbeatable, and she didn't mind hard work.

The one who didn't like hard work was that little hussy of hers. Orchid Ma's web-name was "Heavenly Maiden" but Maddy Yuan, being a realist, came right out and called her "that little hussy." Orchid Ma's head had a nice, round shape, but her thoughts had jagged edges, and she was often a trial to Maddy Yuan. From an early age, Orchid had not shown much special ability, but she went in for silly antics, such as pinning red flowers in her hair or embroidering lovebirds on her jacket. Even so, Maddy Yuan had not fussed about it. When Orchid came to Pei City, her expectations rose a few notches. Maddy Yuan arranged for her to wait tables at a restaurant, but one choice remark from Orchid choked the manager with rage. "It looks like these noodles were boiled with a dishrag. Can people eat these?" Maddy Yuan didn't know what to do with the girl, so she let her stay home and neglected her.

Hua Yuqing liked to watch Maddy Yuan hang his award certificates out to dry. She would remove their red protective covers, exposing the slightly brittle cardstock, and hang them up with clothespins in the gentle breeze. While Maddy Yuan was mopping, Hua Yuqing would bask in the sunlight of a May morning, saying to himself, "This is my historiography award from 2009 ... this was my Certificate of Honor from ten years ago." He would rattle on about how, back in the day, he had done a field survey here in Southtomb, and how he had pored over books day and night. He hadn't let anything dissuade him from pursuing his grand objective. At last, his findings showed conclusively that the occupant of Southtomb had been Prince Jingnan of the Zhou Dynasty. This made him famous overnight, and he was given the "Guo Moruo Gold Cup" Award. Not trying to discourage him, Maddy Yuan would whisk and wipe down all furniture surfaces until the room was spick and span. Sometimes tears trickled down Hua Yuqing's face, and he would ask her why she didn't respond. Maddy Yuan would then nod and say, "I see, I see. But I have to pay the water bill tomorrow, so get the money ready before I leave." In such a way the metaphysical coexisted with the physical, without any major waves being stirred, and both sides got along very well.

When he had free time, Ma Dongqiang also came to Hua's place. Ma Dongqiang was a security guard at Southtomb University. To put things simply, Hua Yuqing had found the job for him. In times like these, finding a campus guard position is not easy. Luckily, Ma Dongqiang had served in the Army, so he knew the basics of hand-to-hand combat. He spent his days sitting in a campus police booth, his face caressed by a spring breeze at the window. Working here was like living in a lotusland. So now and then Ma Dongqiang would come bringing liquor and a choice dish or two, with a carton of Double Happiness cigarettes. He came to visit Hua Yuqing, thinking to chat with him about the *Romance of Three Kingdoms*. Rather than being a show of Ma's gratitude, this was more a display of tolerance on Hua's part. After all, Ma could get a few gilt coins in exchange for such trifles as cigarettes which meant nothing to Hua. A person of character takes a firm stance, like Zhuangzi's praying mantis that defied an oncoming wagon. As for a schemer of dubious character, one could liken him to Zhuangzi's sparrow getting ready to peck the mantis from behind.

On this particular day when Ma Dongqiang dropped by, he came upon a few students from Southtomb University. Ma was a bit ill-at-ease, as if not knowing what to do with his hands and feet. Hua Yuqing did not notice, because his mouth was flapping away. The students nodded, took notes and from time to time asked questions that Ma couldn't understand. Ma put down the things in his hands and plunked himself in a seat anyway. Maddy Yuan dashed into the room and gave him a smack on the head. The group looked up perplexedly, but she just said icily: "Go dress the fish." For Ma Dongqiang, this was the ray of hope he'd been waiting for. He scampered off to the kitchen to scrape fish scales. The conversation in the living room went on for some time. The gist of it was that they would pick Hua Yuqing up two days later and take him to an academic conference. Hua Yuqing gave assent in two syllables: "*Mmm-hmm*." Ma Dongqiang nudged Maddy Yuan with his elbow as he cleaned the fish, leering at her suggestively.

Sure enough, Ma had been salivating over the Hua residence for some time. It was on the 20th floor of a condo building with good light exposure. The sofa was of real leather and the furniture was of rosewood. On top of that was the doughy-soft, heavenly Simmons mattress. Lying on it would be like floating on a cloud in never-never land. Since he had first laid eyes on the Hua residence, Ma had been like a cuckoo sizing up a magpie's nest. Not only that, the magpie would be away from home. Ma silently uttered the words "Well, well, well ..." Well, this was a chance to spend time in never-never land. So it appeared that his bumkin-ish offerings of Double Happiness cigarettes and White Jade liquor had not been a dead loss.

Before two days had passed, Maddy Yuan packed up Hua's suitcase, dressed him in shirt and trousers, and boiled a thermos full of water for his trip. Then Hua cocked his head without saying a word, whereupon she went to the kitchen and fried two eggs. The doctor had said that old people should avoid oily foods, but fried eggs were so easy to make. All she needed to do was pour oil in a pan, crack the shells open, add a dash or two of salt, and before long Hua would be sitting back with a film of yolk on his lips. That's how a person lives from day to day, because who knows what he turns into after death? Hua crooked his body, trying to touch and pull up the top of his socks. Maddy Yuan didn't care. She added another dash of salt, then turned off the exhaust fan as the room filled with the smell of fried eggs, the kind with liquid yolks. Hua ingested a few mouthfuls as Maddy Yuan washed the pan. "What kind of gift would you like?" Maddy Yuan couldn't make out what he said. Hua asked, "What gift would you like?" The pan in Maddy Yuan's hands clanged against the sink and she stopped to think. "Is there cinnamon bark where you are going? Is there white pepper? The stuff those sons of bitches sell in Pei City is not top grade."

En-route between the little flat at 18 Tongriver Road and the condo in Building 8, Springriver Gardens, Orchid Ma skipped and bounced the whole way: as Maddy Yuan saw it, the girl was just being her normal self. As for Ma Dongqiang, who brought up the rear, he had a lot on his mind. Orchid's hair was in pigtails, and her features seemed to have softened quite a bit. Ma Dongqiang carried a large canvas bag over his shoulder, which Maddy Yuan said he had brought to "dig for treasure." But there was a lot of stuff at Hua's house; if one or two articles were subtracted from that clutter, it wouldn't make much difference. Maddy Yuan said to him: "Don't you dare take too much." Ma Dongqiang said, "I've already let him take you, so who cares if I take a little token of kindness from him?"

That night Maddy Yuan slept soundly, but Ma Dongqiang tossed and turned. The Simmons was nice to lie on, but it made him feel he had no backbone. Orchid Ma also lay with her eyes open, looking at the contoured molding around the recessed ceiling. She looked at the many-paned glass doors of the bookcases, with their rows of dark- and light-colored books. This book was called *The Beauty of Baroque*; that one was called *What Does the Starry Sky Bring Us?* They were like a series of swinging rosewood-lattice doors, screened with red gauze; they would swing open at the slightest touch to show filmy clouds hiding the moon; they were graceful like snowflakes whirled by eddies of wind: it was a splendiferous new world.

As Maddy Yuan chased butterflies in her dream, Ma Dongqiang got up and made a circuit around the living room and porch, which brought him to the studio. He had never seen so many books except at the library of Southtomb University. They were like rows of willow leaves tossed in a breeze; they were like decks of old playing cards worn at the edges by many hands.

Hua Yuqing's studio was huge, like a platform for stargazing. Aside from those rows of books, there were shiny trophy cups. Some were of quartz, and some were shiny and golden. They gave off light that reminded him of legendary beauties—like the earrings of Qiao the Elder or spittle from Qiao the Younger's lips. Now Ma Dongqiang was getting impatient. He rapped on this trophy cup and tapped on that one. From the clear, ringing sounds, he knew the pedestals were hollow. What kind of honors were these inscriptions talking about? He rubbed the words with the pads of his fingers: they were deeply incised. His heart fluttered like a pennant. They were his for the next few days. He would have a little drink or two out of them. It would do a man good to have them next to him while he slept. That night in May, a wave of bliss swept over Ma Dongqiang. In the corner of a bookcase he saw something gleaming. He moved closer: it was the Guo Moruo Gold Cup. Ma's eyes were gleaming just like the cup, like Jiang Gan when he stumbled on a hoard of rare books.

The Ma family spent two unforgettable days in the Hua residence. The May weather was slightly hot. Orchid Ma turned up the air conditioning while still wearing a long-sleeved blouse; she leafed through picture books on the table and watched the 42″ LED television, all the while polishing off the supply of milk in the refrigerator. Ma Dongqiang had his own amusement: he luxuriated in the studio with a pair of glasses propped on the bridge of his nose, bobbling his head as he pored over a copy of the *Romance of Three Kingdoms*. Maddy Yuan was not the relaxing type: she bustled about in the kitchen until she came out with dishes to thump on the table saying "Time to eat!"

Before Hua Yuqing returned home, Maddy Yuan had restored the place to its former appearance. Hua Yuqing set down his suitcase, rolling his wheelchair forward, and handed a painting to Maddy Yuan. It was a painting of rapeseed fields, riotous growths of yellow, undulating with the terrain under the sky, pushing against each other and achieving some kind of immortality on the painted surface. Maddy Yuan thanked Hua, then immediately laid it aside; she cast aside his gesture of warm goodwill. Hua said, "You ought to know, that was painted by a folk artisan; the color scheme is excellent." Maddy Yuan just pursed her lips and wiped her oily hands on her apron. Her parents had toiled in rapeseed fields for a lifetime, had gotten no more than a hovel of second-rate bricks.

Maddy Yuan calculated it was the time. She went to Hua Yuqing's bedroom: he was dozing in his chair, his head sinking and then snapping back like a pecking chicken. She wanted to wake him up, but she didn't have a good excuse, so she brought a cleaning rag and flitted about the room, making a raspy sound as she buffed the surfaces. Hua Yuqing awoke with a jolt, held his head high, and looked all about. Seeing Maddy Yuan, he let out an exhalation of relief. She walked over and began rubbing his feet. Hua deflected the embarrassment of the moment by asking if everything was alright. Maddy Yuan kept her head down and answered mutedly. "What about that conversation you said you'd have with Old Zhang, about his son?" "My goodness, I forgot." Hua touched the palm of his hand to his forehead. "I'll go talk to him about it, right away."

Old Zhang's son was

surnamed Zhang, as is only natural. Ma Dongqiang's daughter was surnamed Ma, which only makes sense. *Zhang-Ma, Ma-Zhang*. When you roll the names Ma and Zhang around on your tongue, they go together easily. Maddy Yuan had been harboring this intention for quite some time. Some time back she saw Zhang Honglei on the stairway. His stature was not tall, his physique was a bit pudgy: he looked well-behaved and good-tempered. He wore a set of thin-framed glasses—a studious type. This was just the ticket! Maddy Yuan was satisfied, but what would Orchid think? She didn't give much thought to that. It wouldn't matter if they had sons or daughters, Maddy Yuan just wanted grandchildren, and she wanted them to have some culture.

The powers of heaven like to toy with people's fates. Maddy Yuan had an accident riding her scooter. Her injuries were not life-threatening, but one arm had a bump, and she was lame in one leg. The old woman who had run into her was also riding a scooter. The old woman railed at Maddy Yuan for not using her eyes. Maddy Yuan just sat in the road, rubbing her leg and howling. By this time lots of people were gathering around. The old woman knew her part in this did not look good, so she threw down 500 *yuan* and pushed her scooter through an opening in the crowd. The 500 *yuan* was strewn all over the road. She reached for it and raked it in, not knowing whether to go on crying or smile through the tears.

Hua Yuqing told Maddy Yuan she could take two days off, but she wouldn't agree to that. She earned 180 *yuan* a day, so a day's work could buy her a few ham hocks. And what if some coquettish Jezebel came sashaying in to care for Hua? Maybe Maddy Yuan would be replaced. She was not one to dwell upon the things men and women get up to, but she understood. Years ago, after Ma Dongqiang had done it with her a couple of times, her parents had no choice but to marry her off. She didn't let things bother her: what it boiled down to, in her view, was that whoever you marry, it's a marriage; whatever kind of child you have, she's your child. As long as you make a decent life for yourself, it's alright. She hoped that Orchid Ma would see things the same way.

The buildings in Springriver Gardens had elevators, so Maddy Yuan didn't have to trudge up the stairs. But back at #18 Tongriver Road there was no elevator. It was a building from the '90s, rundown and outdated, with a smell like death warmed over. Each day Maddy Yuan dragged her lame leg on and off her scooter. At some point it had been knocked out of alignment, so it squeaked all the way to Springriver Gardens. When she arrived the scooter made a last plaintive creak, as if waiting for its master's body warmth. She did not make it wait too long. She only had to do simple housecleaning, fill Hua Yuqing's belly, and the 180 *yuan* would be hers. Once her warm rear end sat on the scooter, it seemed to squeak delightedly; neon signs seemed to flash delightedly. As one traffic light after another shone on her face, she thought of the 80 *yuan* that Ma Dongqiang had won at cards yesterday. That would be enough to buy a T-shirt for Orchid Ma. The sky was darkening; the little scooter was skimming along.

Not until a couple of days later did Maddy Yuan notice: aside from going to card games, Ma Dongqiang was showing signs of infatuation. She was pretty sure he wouldn't dare to cast himself in the part of Romeo, so she ignored him. But when she made tea eggs, he nibbled them as if he didn't taste them. Maddy Yuan did not make tea eggs very often, because they required lots of ingredients. So his behavior caused Maddy Yuan to lie awake that night. She kept her eyes half open and held her tongue. Sure enough, Ma Dongqiang got up in the middle of the night, dug about in a cabinet and pulled out a gleaming object. He sprayed it with saliva and polished it with his sleeve. Then he turned on the floor lamp and adjusted it to shine on himself; he stood before the mirror and held the object up. That was the "Guo Moruo Gold Cup" that Hua Yuqing had kept hidden in the dark recesses of a cabinet.

Maddy Yuan had guessed as much at the beginning—Ma Dongqiang had filched it while staying at Hua's place. So she sat up and asked him: "Why did you take it?" Ma answered, "It looks nice." Maddy Yuan said, "Plenty of things look nice. Why don't you steal something from a shopping center?" Ma Dongqiang laughed, grabbed her finger and rubbed it across the pedestal. "Feel that?" The pad of her finger could feel the deeply incised characters; her heart was flapping like a pennant. "Guo Moruo Cup Gold Award," she said aloud as she rubbed it. All the noises outside had died down, and the moon had hidden itself away. Maddy Yuan could hear her own heartbeat.

The laundry on the clothesline made a colorful show on this breezy day. Hua Yuqing looked up; Maddy Yuan was in the kitchen mincing green onions and ginger. Today she had bought a carp caught in the river. The fish seller had given her an extra *yuan* in change. As she thought about this and that, the knife sliced a nick in her finger. Oh well, human blood is blood, just like fish blood. Maddy Yuan eased the carp into hot oil.

This time the carp was done to perfection. It rested in the bowl like a crescent moon with its head and tail tilted upwards. Hua dug his chopsticks into the flesh on its side. The air was alive with the gush and gurgle of Maddy Yuan washing the wok. Suddenly, she heard an odd sound. Turning about, she saw Hua give her a fear-stricken look as he held his hand against his throat.

Hua Yuqing spent a long time in the otolaryngology ward. A dazzling halogen lamp shone on his face, lighting all the furrows and creases of his skin. The clock's second hand seemed to spin about as Maddy Yuan stood looking on helplessly. Hua Yuqing held his mouth open for a long time, until tears started streaming from the corners of his eyes. The forceps clinked repeatedly against his teeth. The doctor said, "Open your mouth wider," and Hua opened wider; the doctor said, "Swallow your saliva," and Hua did as he was told. Maddy Yuan watched, thinking growing old was really something unbearable.

Not long after the fishbone was removed, Hua had visitors from the university. It was the same bunch of students who had come to see him before, this time with bouquets in their hands and restrained smiles on their faces. Hua Yuqing motioned them to sit, chatted with them briefly, then sent them home. The doctor said Hua was good to go. Hua spat up gobs of phlegm, then spoke to Maddy Yuan, with a catch in his voice, "It's stuffy in here. Let's go outside where there's a breeze." It was one of those south winds of early May, like the air in a popcorn popper. Maddy Yuan was about to sigh with relief, but then she saw tears trickling from Hua's eyes. She was about to ask what was wrong, but Hua started talking first. His son Hua Xiaozhi had earned top marks from an early age; he had shown exceptional intelligence. He scored 100s on exams, won prizes, and in every respect followed in his father's footsteps. He was doted on and coddled by both parents, and he justified their expectations, eventually testing into Yale University. Each step of his life seemed to have been pre-arranged to go smoothly. Yet he had an obstinate streak, and after graduation he did not return to China. Hua Yuqing's wife was a frail woman who did not live to enjoy her blessings. And now he himself was paralyzed. For family ties, all he had was an occasional trans-Pacific phone call, and a sum of money that was wired into his account each month. Speaking of this was emotionally painful to Hua, and he started wiping away tears again. "I really envy you," said Hua as he raised his head and sniffed several times. "It's so nice that your whole family is together." Maddy Yuan didn't know what to say, so she showed him the cut on her finger: "That fish was really fierce." Hua Yuqing suddenly started laughing, making a *hmmph-hmmph* sound in his throat. She laughed along with him. Hua pointed to his useless legs, then pointed to her lame leg. The two of them exchanged glances, then burst into gales of laughter.

The little hussy Orchid Ma was dragged off to the Hua residence, even before she had finished braiding her hair. Before the Zhangs showed up,

Hua Yuqing chatted awhile with Orchid Ma and let her look around. Orchid Ma looked around her, at the contoured molding below the recessed ceiling. She looked at the many-paned glass doors of the bookcases, with their rows of dark-and light-colored books. They were like a series of swinging rosewood-lattice doors, screened with red gauze. They would swing open at the slightest touch to show filmy clouds hiding the moon; they were graceful like snowflakes whirled by eddies of wind: it was a splendiferous new world. Having renewed her impressions, she slipped away to the bathroom. She had brought her comb with her, and some rubber bands. Orchid looked at herself in the mirror. There was a new softness and charm in her square face, with its gooseberry eyes and wide ears and heifer-like nose. When her pigtails were braided, she stretched the rubber bands over the back of her hand. She swung her arms and let out a laugh that sounded like tinkling bells.

Old Zhang and his son showed up, and everyone exchanged pleasantries. Maddy Yuan and Old Zhang found excuses to leave Hua's place. That left the erudite old man with the young people. The burden was on him, not just to play the go-between, but to flaunt his knowledge gained in a lifetime. First, Hua introduced Orchid Ma to Young Zhang. "This young woman is warm and kind. You can see that she has clear, dark eyes and delicate eyebrows. Her personality is open-hearted and generous. She is neither a hedonist, nor is she a cold, aloof type. To sum it up, Orchid Ma is a down-to-earth young woman who knows about day-to-day living. In this day and age, I think she's worth holding onto." This had a spell-binding effect on Young Zhang, who could do nothing but nod at every sentence. Then it was time to introduce Young Zhang. Hua Yuqing was just opening his mouth when Orchid Ma butted in: "If a guy's height falls short of 170 cm, isn't that like being a semi-cripple? And you have a lot of fat on your bones: have you thought of going on a diet?

How about your glasses, do they have a high prescription? If you take them off can you see how many fingers I'm holding up?" Each remark was like a sickle blade or axe, cutting an awkward grin on Zhang's face. Hua Yuqing laughed for a moment, not knowing what to say. That little hussy was jiggling her leg, waiting to see what her opponent would throw at her next.

After a moment, Hua Yuqing switched subjects and chatted with Young Zhang about his father. Hua spoke of how Old Zhang used facial tissues, and how he always turned aside when cleaning his nose, and especially, how he washed his hands before playing cards. All of these showed that Old Zhang was not like other people. Young Zhang gradually cheered up and talked about how his father always read books before bedtime, and how he practiced calligraphy every day, and how he raised houseplants that were a sight to behold. The two were trading enthusiastic remarks when Orchid Ma butted in again: "If Old Zhang wants to pick his nose, it would be better if he went somewhere out of sight, you know what I mean? He plays cards, but if his cardplaying skills are as poor as people say, he should feel sorry for his partner. Why humiliate himself? He reads and does calligraphy and raises houseplants: all of those are things that old people do when they're bored." Young Zhang's countenance grew progressively darker, and he gulped down mouthfuls of saliva as he took this in. Seeing that things were not going well, Hua raised himself in his chair and said, "I seem to recall that Old Zhang is planning to practice *taiji* sword today. Don't you want to take your father there?" Young Zhang turned up his eyes at Orchid Ma and took his leave.

The door of the Hua residence closed with a thud. Hua looked at the reddish-brown door and heaved a sigh. For a long time he made slight rotations of his wheels, then he spun all the way around and saw Orchid Ma: square-faced with gooseberry eyes and wide ears and a heifer-like nose, but this time ... she was totally naked.

Hua Yuqing was dumbfounded. Although Orchid Ma could not quite be called a beauty queen, the overall effect of her sculpted contours, her supple and delicate skin, her pert and full breasts were enough to remind him how long it had been since he saw a woman naked. Hua's cheeks were distended from the rush of blood; his eyes were popping out of his head. Orchid Ma walked toward him with hips swinging and breasts undulating. Hua wrenched his head around, trying not to look. Orchid Ma hooked her index finger under his chin and brought his head around. As the flush on his face deepened he shouted, "What are you doing?" Orchid Ma sat down on his inert legs. She unfastened his buckle and started pulling down his pants. Hua pushed back her hand. "What are you trying to do?" Orchid Ma laughingly asked, "Why don't you call me 'Heavenly Maiden'?" Then she released him and pushed his wheelchair on a circuit through the condominium. A few award certificates were still hanging to dry. Orchid Ma had him read them out loud. There were books everywhere—in the living room, bedroom and studio. *The Beauty of the Baroque* is about European baroque art of the Middle Ages. *What the Starry Sky Brings Us?* tells how black holes and celestial bodies influence the earth. When they got to his studio, he explained when and where he had won his awards. Seeing the empty space in the corner of one bookcase gave him a start. At this point, Orchid Ma encircled his neck with her arms. She breathed warm air into his ear and asked, "Am I beautiful?" Hua sucked in his breath: "I tell you, I don't know what you're up to here."

Orchid Ma's laugh tinkled like silver bells. She spun the wheelchair around 360 degrees, giving Hua a passing glimpse of a female torso. Orchid leaned against Hua from behind, her breasts pressing on his shoulders. "Professor Hua, please tell me loud and clear that I am mistress of this house. All of this is mine!"

Orchid Ma fastened the last shirt button. The dark mask of Hua's face was turned away.

"You went too far." Orchid Ma tossed her hair about. "Why too far? Did anything happen?" Hua pounded his fists on the wheelchair's armrests. "I'm going to tell your mother." Orchid Ma braided her hair, using the 42″ LED as a reflective surface; her reflection on the screen had the blush of a ripe peach. "Go ahead and tell her."

Hua Yuqing did not tell anyone. As Orchid Ma had said, maybe nothing happened. The whole thing could be treated as a non-event. Fish and noodles were much the same as before, but Hua told Maddy Yuan he didn't want to eat fish noodles any more. She didn't know what this was all about. She fried eggs for him, but he said the yolks were not well cooked, and they tasted sickeningly salty. Maddy Yuan asked what he wanted to eat. He said he wanted "one leg and four legs," so she fried up mushrooms with pork. He said he wanted to eat nothing but low-calorie food, so she bought raw vegetables and made cold platters. He liked them all, but every day he had new demands. Realizing that something had upset him, she did everything as carefully as she could.

When he had stayed indoors long enough, Hua Yuqing wanted to go out for a spin in his wheelchair. Maddy Yuan helped tidy him up. She bent down to straighten the rolled-over tops of his socks. Without even acknowledging her, Hua propelled himself to the door and shut it behind him with a reverberating thud. Maddy Yuan sat on the sofa and let all her cares fall away.

Before long Hua Yuqing came back with a crestfallen look on his face. Old Zhang didn't want anything to do with him and had instigated the others to stay away from him. Maddy Yuan didn't know if she should be sad or happy over this. Bringing a basin of hot water, she removed his socks and helped him soak his feet. A scrap of old skin wavered in the water, not keeping a fixed shape, like an old man on a remote mountain in traditional Chinese painting. As Maddy Yuan rubbed his feet she thought of beard lichens and dodder vines; she thought of a whole field full of rapeseed flowers. Rapeseed oil has such a nice smell, especially when used to fry fish fillets or fish balls. They have a golden tinge and look like precious objects. Maddy Yuan was starting to miss that smell. In the midst of her daze, Hua Yuqing surprised her with a question: "How is your 'Little Heavenly Maiden' ?" In the shock of the moment, she began to surmise what had happened.

Maddy Yuan awoke to the sight of Orchid Ma making bizarre faces in the mirror. *Hey!* Maddy Yuan snapped, asking what she was doing. "What's it to you?" said Orchid. At that Maddy Yuan's temper flared up: she threw aside the cover, pinched Orchid by the ear and asked what the girl had done to offend Professor Hua. At this Orchid's voice quavered aggrievedly: "Who knows what I have done wrong?" Maddy Yuan pressed her questioning further. Orchid just heaved her shoulders and said, "Maybe I said some things that upset Hua Yuqing." She knew that her daughter was not telling the truth, but seeing the girl in tears, like a bough of spring blossoms in the rain ... and seeing the care she had put into her spring-like appearance, Maddy Yuan let her go. Even if the sky were to fall, this was her precious daughter.

Ma Dongqiang had come home late the night before. One sniff was enough to know he had been out drinking. Maddy Yuan hit him with the flat of her hand. He awoke with a start and growled: "What's wrong with you?" she asked, "When are you going to give back that award cup? If you drag this out too long, it's not going to end well." Ma Dongqiang made a sweeping gesture. "There's no hurry," he said, then turned over as if to sleep some more. She pulled at his ear and roared into it: "What you're doing is theft!" The loud noise made Ma Dongqiang's head spin, as if bells and drums were pounding in his ear. "You stinking bitch, are you asking for a beating?" Maddy Yuan hit him again with the flat of her hand. Ma Dongqiang flew into a rage. He lunged at her and began grappling with her arms and hitting her. Maddy Yuan rubbed her teary face and said, "What have I done to offend you, Ma Dongqiang?" Ma smacked her in the face again. "You're caring for another man's needs, even helping him go to the toilet. I'm sure you've seen everything. Stinking bitch!" Maddy Yuan felt she had been terribly wronged. She grabbed Ma Dongqiang's wrist and sank her teeth into it. "Back then I gave in to you. Otherwise, do you think I'd have had wanted anything to do with the Ma family?"

The little scooter was not squeaking now. The spring light was bright and lovely; winter wheat was ready for harvest. Maddy Yuan's mood was a bit brighter now. In this world there is no hole that cannot be mended. Arriving at Springriver Gardens, Maddy Yuan nimbly dismounted from the scooter. From the way she walked to the elevator, no one would believe she was once lame if he didn't look too closely. Her days would get better in time. Harboring this kind of faith, she opened the door of #2003. Hua Yuqing was sitting on the sofa, his expression dark and rigid as he read from a few sheets of letter paper. Maddy Yuan knew better than to ask, so she tiptoed to the balcony to do some cleaning there. Out of the corner of her eye she saw Hua Yuqing take the sheets of paper and a mobile phone into the studio. She put down her mop and leaned against the door to listen.

Wasting no time on preliminaries, Hua Yuqing erupted: "You students insist on coming to see me all the time. If I so much as have a fishbone pulled out, then you come. From the way it looks, people would think you're being devoted and kind. But I was too personally involved to stay clear-minded." As he rattled on, Miss could catch the gist of what he was saying. The same students who often came to visit had torn to shreds his research on the occupant of the Southtomb. Not only that, they had published their own findings in a journal. Hua Yuqing mindlessly pounded his fists on the desk. There was a noise of books and plaques being thrown about, and his bellowing voice: "I never want you in my house again." Maddy Yuan pressed her ear even closer to the door. Just then Hua Yuqing opened the door to see her crouching there in an eavesdropping position.

"You're fired!"

Maddy Yuan asked if there was a way to make it up to him. Hua turned down the corners of his mouth and said, "Impossible." She clasped her hands together, not knowing what to do with them. "Professor Hua, I beg you." Hua Yuqing turned his head away, saying: "Impossible. I'm going over Jingyang Ridge."[2] Maddy Yuan understood that his mind was made up. Hua Yuqing continued, "All of you people have been tricking me. Those students used tricks to turn people against me. My maid uses tricks to get money. And that trifling girl intended to get her hands on my whole estate." Maddy Yuan said, "You have everything." Hua Yuqing rattled on about how the students had pretended to need his sympathy. "You have everything," said Maddy Yuan. Then Hua got onto the subject of Orchid Ma: "If a person's inborn character is low and cheap, she can never change." To this Maddy Yuan said, "You have everything." Hua's voice became more strident, saying that only he and Maddy Yuan had access to his condo. When time came for the police to investigate the whereabouts of his "Guo Moruo Gold Cup," everything would be made clear. "Isn't there another way to deal with this?" sobbed Maddy Yuan. "*Hmph*," he grunted dismissively. "If you borrow something, you have to return it; if you steal something, you go to prison. Even a three-year-old child knows that." Then he went into his spiel about how he had come to Southtomb. He had done field studies and pored over books day and night, letting nothing turn him back from his grand objective. Finally he had established that the nobleman interred at Southtomb was Prince Jingnan of the Zhou Dynasty. "You have everything," said Maddy Yuan. This time the words came out in a long, lamenting tone, trailing off into a wail.

Before Hua Yuqing knew

what was happening, Maddy Yuan had wound tape around his arms and body. He was thoroughly pinned down; even his fingers were bound to the armrests of his wheelchair. With a cold laugh, she looked at his legs. "No need to use it there." Hua Yuqing's eyes were wide-open in terror, and veins stood out at his temples. The duct tape over his mouth was puffed out by the force of his breath. "Is there anything more to say?" asked Maddy Yuan. She peeled the tape from his mouth and, before he could cry out, pressed another piece in place more firmly. Hua's face was crimson, as if to utter a string of obscenities. "There's no need to worry," she said, patting his shoulders. "Old Zhang won't come looking for you. Your students won't come looking for you. Your son won't come looking for you either. You can just sit quietly here and wait for fish soup."

Hua Yuqing started making a low, mournful sound. Maddy Yuan ignored him. She went through the rooms gathering useful things. She pulled out items from the maid's cabinet, including the oil painting that Hua had given her—an expanse of golden-yellow rapeseed flowers. Maddy Yuan thought of tearing it up, but she decided to stuff it in her bag. Her parents had toiled in rapeseed fields all their lives, but they only ended up with a hovel of second-rate bricks. Maddy Yuan took award certificates down from the clothesline and let them fall on Hua's face. Hua was fatigued from his struggles: he watched intently as she rummaged about, tied up a package and then opened the door to leave. When only one crack of the outside world remained, Maddy Yuan's head reappeared and spat out: "You miserable creature ..." Hua Yuqing made no response. He merely looked at the yellowed irises of her eyes, where Prince Jingnan of the Zhou Dynasty, having crawled out from Southtomb, was stalking toward him with a smiling face.

2016

››› Translator's Notes:

1. A second-level professor is a title used in Chinese academic settings for professors who have received a relatively high level of recognition from the accrediting authority.

2. In the classical novel *Along the Water Margin*, the hero Wu Song stopped at a tavern beneath Jingyang Ridge. He was told that a man-eating tiger had killed several people on the ridge recently. Wu Song resolved to cross the ridge despite the danger.

Bluestone Alleys

Fei Zhenzhong / 费振钟
Translated by Josh Stenberg

Without going down one of these little streets in any little Jiangnan[1] town or village, you cannot claim to have set foot in Jiangnan.

These little alleys are mostly paved in bluestone. As to the length or the width of these little alleys—you needn't bother about that; direct your attention instead to the rounded, mottled stones. You can imagine, you can reckon the passing of time over each stone, then add your own footsteps from moments ago to the total—that way you'll be sure to keep a memory of these bluestone alleys in your heart.

You must take note of the high, grey walls of brick on either side, note the rain-soaked crevices between the bricks, not to mention the dabs of moss in the crevices and the handfuls of dark green grass blades. The seclusion of these little alleys is not determined by their length, but by the mottled traces left on them over the years. As you walk down some such little street, and just as you stretch out your hand to stroke the wall, the street will provoke lingering, expansive melancholy and a sigh of emotion, born from a sense of the vicissitudes of time. That's why the little alley never loses its hold upon your footsteps, slowing your walk; and through the leisureliness of your steps, you will find a fateful attachment arising between you and the little alley.

Also take note of the gateway arches facing onto the little street. Perhaps these arches feature a stone lion or two—but it is certain that pictures in relief feature on the brick. These are called brick carvings, and they are not for decoration alone, frequently they have become a guide to the alley, offering passersby painstaking wonderment or surmise. Arches like these feature pitch-black, wooden doors, always tightly shut, and no one can tell you whose archway it is, who has been able for so long to present the life and style of an older era, whose archway seems desirous to open wide, only then to draw back, jealous of its silence and secrets. But as long as you have posed the question, your sentiments towards the little alley will deepen.

Perhaps in some alleys you will also notice the bluestone guards around the wells. It hardly matters whether beneath them the water has gone dry or is abundant. What you must do is look time and again at each of the ruts left by ropes on the well guards, running—always at a particular angle—across the bluestone. You know that these ruts are the traces of years upon years, but you do not know which of these ruts was etched by the tender white hands of a young woman, and which by the calloused fingers of an elderly woman. Some portion of the details of over a century of daily life are carved into this wellguards' bluestone. What is profound about it is also what is indistinct; the days were all thoughtlessly worn away by a rope pulling a wellbucket. How could one ever learn which bucketload of water was used to make tea or distill wine, which to wash the vegetables or to cook, which for sprinkling on the floor before sweeping, which for cleaning? It is not because you are too superficial to understand; rather, it is because your eyes cannot see through the tedium and trivia of mundane life.

And now, I am sure you should direct your attention to the old lady sitting in the little alley. Naturally, she is drawing her hair into the bun just as she has ever since she married into this alley, and naturally she is wearing the blue cotton blouse she has worn ever since she became one of its daughters-in-law, and naturally she is wearing a jade bracelet, which may well be the most important memento she has of her clan and family. You see how at her side there may be an embroidery frame, and her hand might be holding a threaded embroidery needle, working on a piece of never-to-be-completed embroidery. That's why the old lady and her embroidery, too, will become an immutable part of this little alley's tale. You pass in front of the old woman, maybe even carrying this tale away with you.

By the time you're done walking down the little alleyway, the sky above is darkening. The high firewalls and the vines that creep upon them cast their shadows over the bluestones. Treading on the alleyway's shadows, what more do you seek?

Later, in the street corner, a lamp is lit. Later, after you have left, the alley sinks into its lonely dream.

››› Translator's Notes:

1. Jiangnan, meaning "south of the river," is the district and historic cultural area of the lower reaches of the Yangtze river.

Rain in the Old Village

Fei Zhenzhong / 费振钟
Translated by Josh Stenberg

Not many villages like this one are left. Their disappearance, day by day, is all but inevitable. Even with the imposition of painstaking protections, these villages can't resist the power of time. Of course, there are still a few old villages in Jiangsu, Zhejiang and Anhui, but it is evident that they have lost all connection with their environments. They exist in the manner of a taxidermist's specimen. There they are, exhibited, with every tile, every stone, right down to every tree testifying to stasis, to stagnation.

Around the city of Jinhua in Zhejiang province, one might travel to Zhuge Bagua village, or also to Changle Village, or Guodong village, or some other village. You needn't choose between them, they all cut the same taxidermic figure. Alright, Guodong Village—Guo Hollow— it is.

At the entrance to Guodong Village, we can see the village's former name. That name now seems very ancient and elegant, since it translates as "Double-Spring Old *li*," with *li* translating perhaps as "hamlet." In what era were villages known as *li*? It must precede the Han or Tang Dynasties. That would make Guodong Village over two thousand years old, if it is old enough for that term to have been in use. It also has the "Double-Spring" as its symbol; so, how long have the spring waters been flowing here?—the village may be as old as the springs themselves, though that's the sort of thing that requires expert investigation before it can be cleared up.

Guodong Village is representative of the general pattern for villages of historical record. The village are enclosed by drystone walls, and you must pass through a stone gate in order to enter the village. This functions as the village's strategic pass, speaking not only to the way the village cut itself off with ramparts for the sake of safety, but also the enclosed way of village life. The village's connections with the outside world are discrete, and a kind of battened-down, conservative attitude is everywhere retained in consideration of their self-sufficient way of life. Another aspect of village seclusion is furnished by the luxuriating trees outside the walls, with no paucity of thousand-year-old camphor trees, scholar trees, elms, and pines, whose timeless seclusion of the village steeps the village deeper into an atmosphere of yore. It is a type of seclusion that is aesthetic, idealistic, utopian, calling to mind the Peach Blossom Spring of Wuling[1]. Surrounded by ancient trees, with wildflowers slipping into the flowing spring waters, and only a small gate ensuring connection to the outer world—isn't that the paradigm of the Peach Blossom Spring? No wonder the name of this village means Guo Hollow, or, in the words of Tang poet Zhang Xu, "a hollow somewhere at the stream's verdant verge." If an outsider wanted to enter the village, wouldn't he have to cast about, looking for the concealed channel?

Yet we have no difficulty at all in entering the village, and its situation does not resemble Peach Blossom Spring. Inside is a complex of meticulously constructed Ming and Qing style residential buildings, by and large walled in white and tiled in grey, with a stretch of high straight linked firewalls carving up the heavens above the village, and beneath it the narrow alleyways, alleyways connecting the doors of every village household. Because these doors are permanently closed, the alleys seem void and forlorn, and so we can see, to borrow the words of Tao Yuanming, "houses of a stately appearance" , but no sign of a life in which "the white-haired and children are merry together." Dwelling secluded behind high walls and heavy doors no doubt further augments the village mystery. Thus, we can only let our gaze linger on the village's outward appearance. We pass among the buildings, always reflecting on the unitary style developed over a century or two, giving voice to our heartfelt admiration for the unique and intense sense of form evinced in the village's residential style. Our fingers point at the garden windows, set in myriad patterns in the white walls, the brick carvings inlaid in every gateway arch, not to mention the countless ornamental wood engravings—and we fully understand that every one of these has come into being through the careful conception of a master workman, that the villagers' secluded lifestyle and solitary cast of mind have been decorated with an exterior layer of "art," making use of these delicate classical forms to store up their hermetically sealed ideals of living. Perhaps, in this way, we carelessly stroll into the quintessence of the village.

In fact, ever since the area has attracted outside tourist attention, the village's functions have withered day by day. Its value is no longer to be found in its life, which has been reduced to an object of appreciation. Even the village itself has been enlisted in the ranks of admirers, appreciating, along with outsiders, its own seclusion. It is as though this century or two of delicate carvings and engravings have passed simply to meet today's need to gaze and admire. The village is letting itself become an ancient *objet d'art*, allowing its accents and attitudes to collude in this effort, winning a reputation for and the appreciation due to "culture." For that reason, it will not overtly seek to bar the entry of outsiders, going not only to show that it can't compare with the Peach Blossom Spring, but also that it is in contradiction with its quintessential seclusion. For that reason, we will see in the end that people in such villages are no longer as secluded as formerly, and so will move outside the village. Without a sound, without an expression of life, without the daily activities of life, the village will transform into an empty shell, a ruin. At this point, the village will acquire the appellation of "culture" and be named an "original ecology village." Outsiders come for some kind of culture, ramming right in, poking their heads in everywhere; and when they feel satiated they return to modern life, emitting a few belches redolent of culture.

Only that spring morning, when the heavens above the village released a drizzle, and on the stone roads of the village an old peasant wearing a straw rain cape and a bamboo hat led the only plough buffalo out, trailing the sound of damp hooves behind it—only then was the village truly real enough to move us a little deeper.

››› Translator's notes:

1. The Peach Blossom Spring, imagined by the 5th century poet Tao Yuanming (陶渊明), has remained an enduring utopian archetype. Cut off from the outside world, the inhabitants of the Peach Blossom Spring live in peaceful harmony.

Poems

Poems by Hu Xian

Hu Xian / 胡　弦
Translated by Simon Patton

Hu Xu / 胡弦

卵石

——那是关于黑暗的
另一个版本：一种有无限耐心的恶，
在音乐里经营它的集中营：
当流水温柔的舔舐
如同戴手套的刽子手有教养的抚摸，
看住自己是如此困难。
你在不断失去，先是坚硬棱角，
接着是光洁、日渐顺从的躯体。
如同品味快感，如同
在对毁灭不紧不慢的玩味中已建立起
某种乐趣，滑过你
体表的喧响，一直在留意
你心底更深、更隐秘的东西。
直到你变得很小，被铺在公园的小径上，
经过的脚，像踩着密集的眼珠……
但没有谁深究你看见过什么。岁月
只静观，不说恐惧，也从不说出
万物需要视力的原因。

Pebble

— Another edition on the subject
of darkness: an evil with infinite patience
manages in music its very own concentration camp:
as the tongues of running water gently lick you with a flow
like an executioner's well-bred, gloved caresses,
it gets more and more difficult to keep an eye on yourself.
Your loss is constant: first, the hard edges go;
then, the smooth body, that daily grows
more docile. It's like savouring a pleasure
or establishing delight in the leisurely contemplation
of annihilation, and the clamour
that glides over your surfaces is always noticing
deeper and more secret things in your inner being,
until you shrink in size and are paved
in the path of some public park
where feet pass over you, as if they were treading
on densely packed eyeballs ...
No one, however, has taken the trouble to find out
what exactly it is you've seen. The years
mindfully observe, neither speaking of horror,
nor ever giving any reason for why all other creatures
have a need for the power of sight.

马戏团

不可能一开始就是锣，
一开始就是猴子和铃铛。

狗熊裹着皮大衣，心满意足，

Circus Troupe

You can't expect gongs right from the start,
or monkeys and small bells.

A black bear wrapped in a leather coat is perfectly content,

理想主义的鹿却有长久的不宁。
不可能一开始就是铁笼子，
就是算术、雪糕、绕口令。

不可能一开始马就是马，
狮子就是狮子；不可能
一开始就到了高潮，就宣称
没有掌声无法谢幕。

不可能一开始就和气一团；
就把头伸进老虎嘴里。
观众鼓掌，打唿哨，连猎人
也加入了进来。不可能一开始
猎人就快乐，老虎也满意。

撒旦酣睡，艺术驯良，
天使从高处忧心忡忡飞过。
在这中间是马戏团的喧哗。
不可能一开始就这么喧哗。

不可能一开始就是火圈、
糖果、道德的跳板；
金钱豹，不可能一开始就爱钱；
头挂锐角的老山羊，不可能
一开始就是素食主义者。

but the deer of Idealism suffers prolonged anxiety.
You can't expect iron cages from the word go,
or arithmetic, ice-cream, or tongue-twisters.

Nor can you have horses just as they are,
or lions as lions for that matter. You can't jump
to the climax right from the very beginning, or declare
that there'll be no encore without applause.

You can't be on good terms right from the very start,
or put your head in the tiger's mouth.
The audience claps its hands, whistles — even the hunters
join in, but you can't expect them to be happy,
or the tiger to be satisfied, from the word go.

Satan is fast asleep; Art, tame,
while angels fly high overhead laden with worries.
In between the pandemonium of the troupe resounds.
You can't expect that pandemonium from the very start.

You can't expect rings of fire from the word go, either,
or sweets, or the springboard of morality:
you can't expect golden leopards to love gold
right from the start, or — from the word go —
the old goat with its sharp horns to be a vegetarian.

沙漠

——这从消逝的时间中释放的沙，
捧在手中，已无法探究发生过什么。
每一粒都那么小，没有个性，没有

Desert

— These sands set free from containment in a vanished time:
cup them in your hands, but it's too late to work out exactly
what happened. Every grain is so small, so lacking

记忆，也许
能从指缝间溜走的就是对的。

in individuality, so devoid of memory —
perhaps, then, it is fit that they slip through our fingers.

狂热属于革命，无边荒凉属于失败者。
只有失去在创造自由，并由
最小的神界定它们的大小。而最大的风
在它们微小的感官中取消了偏见。

Fanaticism belongs to revolution, the endless wasteland,
to losers. Only through loss is freedom created,
and the smallest gods delimit their size. The strongest winds,
on the other hand, abolish prejudice
from their miniscule sense organs.

又见大漠，
又要为伟大和永恒惊叹。
而这一望无际的沙，却只对某种临时性感兴趣。
沙丘又在地平线上移动。任何辉煌，最后，
都由这种心灰意懒的移动来完成。

Here again we see the Great Desert,
and again marvel at both its grandeur and eternity,
but this expanse of endless sand is only interested
in provisionality. Dunes shift on the horizon.
Any brilliance is ultimately brought to its completion
by this depressing-dismal shifting.

云

Clouds

云在天上飘来飘去，变来变去，
我们说它像什么什么，其实，
我们和云都知道，云
从来就不是那样的东西。

They drift back and forth across the sky,
shifting shape. We say they look like this
or that, but in fact the clouds know full well —
just as much as we do — that they simply aren't like that.

云一直从事着这样的工作，
不愿在某个造型里久留。
有些越飘越高像永不再回来，有些
则越压越低，进入尘世。
但你很难置身其中，总是转眼间，云

Clouds have always been engaged in the one line
of work: never willing to remain shut up within one mould
for long. Some of them drift higher and higher,
as if they would never come back. Some
sink lower and lower, till they pass into
this mortal world of dust. But you'd be hard pressed

就从某个角色里抽身而去。

to put yourself inside one: always, in the blink of an eye
clouds manage to extricate themselves
from any one fixed role.

自得其乐，呆在具体化的边缘。
多数时候是轻柔的，偶尔从其中
传出雷鸣，和自我解构时难以
消化掉的闪电。
偶尔的，排出整齐鳞片，像一只
巨大的怪兽突然出现在天际。

Content with their lot, they stay on the borders
of the concrete. Mostly gentle, occasionally they transmit
from within peals of thunder, as well as the lightning
they find so hard to digest in their auto-deconstruction.
Occasionally, too, they line themselves up in neat rows
of scales, looming on the horizon
like some enormous sudden monster.

造访

Visiting Acquaintances

……一次意外的造访，
刀子说，经过这里就顺便
来看看你。

... An unscheduled visit: Knife explains: *I just happened to be passing*
so I thought I'd drop in.

刀子的话里没有锋芒，
“打搅打搅！”刀子离去时，
明亮的刃，投来一道抱歉的目光。

There's nothing cutting
in Knife's conversation. *I've taken up*
too much of your time! As it leaves an apologetic gleam glitters
the length of its shiny blade.

刀子是许多人的老朋友，
对生活一直所需不多，比如，
只要别人身上一块模糊的伤疤。

Many claim Knife as a close friend.
It has never asked too much of life, just as long
as there's an indistinct scar somewhere
on every body.

——从不感知疼痛，甚至，
没有耐心听完一声尖叫，刀子
已抽身离去。

— It has never felt pain; it doesn't
even have the patience to wait for the screaming to die down.
By the time that happens, Knife is well and truly
off and away.

蜘蛛

它忙碌、饿、短视，一直
凭借对震动的感觉觅食。

总在修补，网，太容易被毁掉。
树在摇晃，柱子不坚定，
暴风雨总会不期而至。

它有八条腿，但终其一生，生活
从不曾有过八个方向。
——实际上，它吃得并不多，
吐出的粘液，
早已超出了内脏的重量。

提心吊胆，用尽手段捕杀。
荒凉角落里，这些
心藏毒液的家伙像一滴滴阴影，
敏捷地滚来又匆匆消失。

Spider

It is hectic, starving, short-sighted, and forever
dependent on vibration for its food.
Repair is its constant work: a spider's web
is so easily ruined: trees sway, uprights prove unsteady,
storms happen without warning, out of the blue.

Although it has eight legs, life has never had eight directions
for as long as it has lived.
— actually, it doesn't eat that much,
and the sticky saliva it spits already exceeds
the total weight of its internal organs.

On tenterhooks, it does everything in its power
to catch and kill. In neglected corners, these
little devils — hearts filled with poison — look like pin-pricks
of shadow, trundling nimbly down
before they beat a swift retreat.

路

它受命成为一条路，
受命成为可以踏上去的现实。
它拉紧脊椎扣好肋骨因为人多，车重。
当大家都散了，它留在原地。
在最黑的夜里，它不敲任何人的门。
它是睡眠以外的部分，

Road

It was commissioned to become a road,
to become a reality that could be stepped on.
Because of the hordes of people as well as heavy trucks,
it drew in the vertebrae of its spine
and buckled up its ribs.
When everyone goes away, it stays where it is.
On the darkest of nights it knocks on nobody's door.
It is the part sleep leaves out,

它是穿越喧嚣的孤寂，
比阶级直，比尘埃低，比暴政宽，
身上
印满谵妄的脚印。
当它受命去思考，蟋蟀开始歌唱。
它废弃时，万物才真正朝两侧分
开，一半
不知所踪；另一半
伴随它的沉默并靠向
时间的尽头。

a loneliness that cuts a way through the noise and the fuss,
straighter than class, more lowly than dust, broader
than tyranny,
covered all over in delirium's foot prints.
And when it is commissioned to think,
crickets start chirping, but only when
it is taken out of service are things
truly divided either side of it: those on one side
vanish into thin air, while those on the other
accompany its silence and lean towards
time's very end.

琥珀里的昆虫

Insects in Amber

它懂得了观察，以其之后的
岁月。
当初的慌乱、恐惧，一种慢慢凝固
的东西吸走了它们，
甚至吸走了它的死，使它看上去
栩栩如生。
"你几乎是活的"，它对自己说，
"除了
不能动，不能一点点老去，一切都
和从前一样"。
它奇怪自己仍有新的想法，并谨
慎地
把这些想法放在心底以免被吸走
因为
它身体周围那绝对的平静不能
存放任何想法。
光把它的影子投到外面的世界如
同投放某种欲望。
它的复眼知道无数欲望比如

They have learned how to observe
in all the years left to them. After the initial
panic and terror, a slowly congealing substance
sucked them away. It even sucked away
their death, leaving them absolutely lifelike.
It's almost as if you're alive, they say to themselves.
Apart from being unable to move, or grow
gradually older, everything is the same as it was before.
They surprise themselves with the fact that they
continue
to have ideas — cautiously, they hide these ideas,
in case they too are sucked away, because
no idea can be stored in the complete tranquillity
that encloses their bodies.
Light throws their shadows into the outside world
as if it were throwing in some desire.
Their compound eyes know countless desires: for
example,
that a ladder is always placed beneath their immobile

总有一把梯子被放到它不能动的脚爪下。
那梯子明亮、几乎不可见，缓缓移动并把这
漫长的静止理解为一个瞬间。

claws.
That ladder is shiny, almost invisible, and it moves so slowly
this long-drawn-out stasis comes to be understood
as a single instant.

树

树下来过恋人，坐过
陷入回忆的老者。
没人的时候，树冠孤悬，
树干，像遗忘在某个事件中的柱子。
有次做梦，我梦见它的根，
像一群苦修者——他们
在黑暗中呆得太久了，
对我梦中的光亮感兴趣。
——不可能每棵树都是圣贤，我知道
有些树会死于狂笑，另一些
会死于内心的自责声。所以，
有的树选择秘密地活着，把自己
同另外的事物锁在一起；
有的，则在自己的落叶中行走，学会了
如何处理多余的激情。

Trees

Beneath them, lovers have wandered, and the aged
have sat, sunk in memory,
but when there is no one around
their crowns hang suspended in isolation, while their trunks
look like columns forgotten in some incident.
Once I saw their roots in a dream
where they resembled assemblies of ascetics —
they have stayed too long in the dark,
and show an interest in the light of my visions.
— No, not every tree can be a saint. I know
that some die in fits of maniacal laughter, and that others
pass away to the self-reproach of their inner monologues.
For this reason, some choose to live out their lives
in secret, locking themselves together
with other objects, while others walk out
in a shower of falling leaves of their own, having learnt
how to deal with superfluous passion.

影子

——沉默而平静。间或，
用猛烈的摇晃

Shadow

— Quiet and calm. Occasionally,
with a violent agitation,

表达不属于自己的焦灼。

当你沉思，它谦逊地
陪着你沉思。
有时则拉长，拉长，像你留在
生活中的把柄。
但从没有谁能抓住它，
当你起身，它立即
从复杂的境况中抽身离去。

随时变形，并用变形
保留一种很难被理解的真实。
追逐光对你的
每一种叙述；触摸世界以其
万物难以觉察的手，

不被注意，但从未离开，只是你
并不知道这意味着什么。

偶尔，会用突然的变形迎面出现，
吓你一跳。
而当你朝它问询或吼叫，
它坚持认为：
有声音的事物都是荒谬的。

it expresses an anxiety not its own.

When you are lost in thought, modestly
it loses itself along with you.
Sometimes, it stretches, stretches, until
it resembles a handle
you leave behind in the world,
but one that no one has ever taken hold of.
When you stand up, it extricates itself at once
from such complex circumstances.

It changes shape as occasion demands and,
by doing so, retains a truth that defies comprehension.
It pursues every story
the light tells about you, and touches the world
with hands the myriad creatures struggle to detect.

It goes unnoticed, but has never left — only you
have no real idea about what this means.

Now and then, it will charge straight at you
by means of an abrupt shape-changing
that jumps you out of your skin,
but when you question it or bellow at it,
it persists in the view
that anything endowed with a voice is merely ridiculous.

光

案上的蜡烛，守着一寸寸矮下来
　　的光。
对于煎熬，灯笼从不开口，对于
要在大风中不停地晃来晃去，

Light

The candles on the table stand guard over a light
shrinking inch by inch. About suffering
the lantern never says a word, while faced with
constant buffeting by the wind it tightly hugs

它抱紧内心里烧不完的寂静。
而盲者、脊背油亮的搬运工、从医院的座椅上
起身时眼前一黑的人……
你怎样把光递给他们?
悲伤慢于闪电,慢于石头的纹理,和一个在巷道里
爬行的少年。而火车在加速,飞快地
穿过隧道,钢轨上,溅起的火星硬如砂粒。而在
遥远乡间的祖屋里,父亲为了省钱,天黑后,
迟迟不肯打开电灯的开关,
——他习惯了黑暗,并把一只悬浮在
空中的灯泡,教导成了长夜的亲人。

the tranquillity inside that will never stop burning.
But what of blind people, of porters with their smooth shiny backs,
and of those who see darkness in front of their eyes
when they get up from their seats in hospital?
How will you pass on any light to them?
Sadness is slower than lightning, than the veins
in a piece of stone, than a young man crawling through
a mine shaft. The train, in contrast, picks up speed, zooming
though tunnels, along steel rails, raising sparks
hard as grains of sand. Meanwhile,
in his ancestral home far off in the country, a father
puts off switching on the lights when it's dark
to save money — he's grown accustomed to blackness, and
has taught a solitary light-bulb suspended mid-air
to be a close relative to the long, drawn-out night.

砧板上的鱼

……你全部的痛苦构成一条
砧板上的鱼:嘴
张了又张,呼喊在那里形成一个
喑哑黑洞,许多词急速旋转着
在其中消失。

Fish on a Chopping Block

... The sum of your pain goes to compose
a fish on a chopping block: mouth
opening wider and wider, screams there forming
a mute black hole, galaxies of words
spiralling at top speed
and vanishing into it.

Art

Coffee Pot or Water Jug?

Shen Li / 沈　黎

Lin Fengmian (林风眠 1900–1991) paints still life in a class of his own. He would not have sought grandeur in theatrical narrative as Philippe Rousseau did in *Chardin and His Models* (1867). He would not have dragged a pair of battered boots into his frame as van Gogh did in *A Pair of Shoes* (1886), nor would he have used an asparagus tip as the single motif like Manet (*Asparagus*, ca. 1880). Lin is drawn to glassware, its glistening transparency being a source of zestful inspiration. Glass vessels are often put in company with ceramic and terracotta pots and vases for comparison and contrast, albeit there is no intent to bring the different textures to finish. These items are subject to a variety of deployment, akin to Parisian homes, modest but ritzy all the same.

Nonetheless, Lin was not a happy scene shifter with all the inventory at his disposal. In 1938, when most regions in China were war-stricken, he had to leave his comfortable home in Hangzhou for the city of Chongqing, where he stayed through 1945 in exile. Next to a tattered warehouse located on the southern bank of Jialing River (嘉陵江), he found a farmhouse that had a small storage shed on offer. Bare with clay walls and mud floor, his lodging was anything but the graceful interiors to be depicted in his still life. Ill-equipped, he had to swerve from oil painting to Chinese ink painting, a medium not quite amenable to the genre of still life.

When the condition was at its starkest, it was only natural for him to miss his home back in Hangzhou, admirably exquisite, so much so that many of his students were eager to have a look at. To create a comfort zone, however restricted, was an effort to deliver a bit of solace to him. No longer serving as mere ornate props, Han-styled or Venetian-styled, placed in the boudoir in his lady paintings, each and every object started to breathe in its own right. Calm daily scenes, when modeled with style, could help the painter rise above the real for the ideal as he did in landscapes and lady-paintings. He was aligned with the modern

Chardin and His Models 1867
Philippe Rousseau

A Pair of Shoes 1886
Vincent van Gogh

Asparagus ca. 1880
Edouard Manet

view that the power of art does not lie in subject matter itself, be it a tarnished coffee pot or a bunch of wild flowers gathered fresh from the field, but in the effect it produces.

This spirit is set alight in Lin's still-life oeuvre, simple yet charming. He has a taste for green fruit, especially pears, rendered mostly unfinished, low-key in tonality, a treatment evoking Cézanne's apples, celebrated for the grim air wallowing across the canvas. Aside from a few cues that can be gleaned from the shape and color, the fruit could be pear, lime, lemon, or even quince if you like. Lin thrives on orchestrating a rhythmic spatial relationship. Of a handful of his favorites, a glass fruit bowl often comes forth with a stout vase of flowers, with a slim jug slipped in between for balance. Anecdotes abound about some seventeenth-century Dutch painters who went to great lengths to borrow priceless objects such as Etruscan pottery, Wanli (万历, 1573–1620) porcelain, and Venetian glassware from their rich friends in order to allure audience. Lin has never followed suit thanks to his confidence in using a lucid language to conjure up a spectacle from a simple way of modeling things. Not working on commission has allowed him to take off further in his own direction.

Whether it is possible to go modern and still be Chinese has been a question nagging him throughout his career. Apart from following the convention of painting objects from close quarters, he explored in a range of dimensions. His successful fusion of ink brushwork with a broad palette has made his still life poles apart from his Western counterparts, classic and modern alike. Much of the punch owes to a refined and protean execution of ink, especially in lining. Meanwhile, his prowess in linear drawing, either with a hefty ink-brush or a tiny hog-brush, converges with the modernist attempt to absorb skills of vivid lining from chinoiserie and ukiyoe. What Lin has relished is a vision appealing directly to the eye. For arrangement, three pieces—a fruit bowl, a water jug, and a vase of flowers—are shuffled and reshuffled to capture a mood emergent at the moment. Whether the array is displayed on a wood table or marble-topped ledge, whether the surface is round or oval, whether everything is placed in a kitchen or elsewhere, are rarely handled with a sense of ceremony, undoubtedly an act of avowed modernism.

Not *de rigueur* to follow the conventional rectangular format, known as the golden mean, Lin has chosen to work on a square format—sixty-eight by sixty-eight centimeters—that has eventually settled as his signature style not only for his still life but for the other genres he straddles. The square format is primed to compare with the curvy and arched lines traveling with brio. Ink brushwork is seen barging into water colors mixed with gouache and vice versa. The spell of "you can't" is broken by deftly appropriating the aliens into intimate allies. Grayish ink is applied to the outline of green fruit and delicate white gouache to the fringe of glassware for a pithy emphasis of the pristine transparency.

He has repeatedly returned to the beloved motifs to exploit their spatial relationship to great effect. Whether planned or not, serial variations have come on the scene. Yet the problem is that most of his early works are truly untitled, utterly different from the practice of some Expressionist artists who would provide a serial number to avoid confusion, for instance, *Untitled No. 1* as opposed to *Untitled No. 5*. For the job of labeling, there is no better choice for editors than generically calling most of his still-life paintings *Still Life* and most of his lady paintings just *Lady* or *Ladies* if in plural. When it comes to the year of production, there is no way to go beyond "ca. 1940s" or "ca. 1950s" for exact labeling. It is hard to tell the works produced during the wartime from the postwar period, and it is hard, for that matter, to figure out the initial version from the variant.

To tackle the issue, let's look at three 1940s serial variations printed in *Lin Fengmian: Collected Works* (Sichuan Fine Arts Publisher, 1994). As is known, the print that comes first in the volume is not necessarily the true original. Obviously, there is no chronological order available for the works produced within the span of 1940s. When opinion overrides fact, what is supposedly produced circa 1940s could be relabeled if controversy ever arose. In the present case, the timeline set by the editors for the serial variations shows a speculation about increasing simplicity in Lin's process of creation.

The first print (Print 1) looks complicated with sturdy ink lines crisscrossing full-frame. Dominant in the foreground are green-fruit hodgepodges piled up in a glass bowl. Positioned behind it is a large bouquet of yellow gladioli thrust randomly in a murky vase, modeled somewhat remotely after the stout jars made in the span of the Han Dynasty (206 BC–220 AD) that Lin has admired. Yellow gouache is applied to the vivacious petals with a few accenting oranges. Dark cobalt green, several levels darker than the pear-like fruit, runs through the bouquet's stalks. Next to the fruit bowl stands a tall and slim water jug or simply a jug functioning as ornament, glazed with umber-and-white stripes. The narrow whites succumb to the strength of chunky umbers. Opposite and complementary effects are exerted in terms of color and shape.

With shafts of sunlight pouring in from the wall-to-wall windows, it looks like a moment of spring-burst, at least metaphorically for the delightful tabletop. Needless to say, the sun-lit sentiment can do nothing to help claim the painting as the initial version. Clueless as ever, several lines, busy and uncertain, can prompt a wild guess of the painting as a sort of study to be deepened, if not abstracted. This guesswork seemingly dovetails with the editors' speculation about the work as the initial.

Ten pages later, the trio reappears, morphed in a number of aspects, though. Cast in large part by depressing shadows, the second print (Print 2) can hardly be read as a moment waking to the morning sun, contented. It utters a melancholic mood that exiles like Lin are prey

Still Life (Print 1) ca. 1940s
Lin Fengmian

to. Attention is immediately drawn to the potted flowers, chrysanthemum-like. Unusually sparse, its yellow petals are poised in animated motion, comparable to van Gogh's energetic sunflower petals. Presumably, the petals endure because of the opportunity of bathing in the sunlight rationed for the single window the pot stands against. When air-raid sirens were no "wolf-calls" subject to rationing of any kind, there is a likelihood that the yellows might be the last dregs squeezed out of the tube—an alert raised for immediate rationing of watercolor tubes, paper, and all. To treat the

Still Life (Print 2) ca. 1940s
Lin Fengmian

flowers at the ending yet enduring stage seems to be doing double duty: an economic use of yellow and a vivid dramatization of the lingering petals. Moreover, rays of light, rain or shine, need to be brought in for the sake of hope. This imposing move of rationing is far more crucial to survival than meagerly rationed food. Then what if the painting is not a wartime work? Void of any hard fact, it sounds safe to zip away the counterargument and let the self-referential symbol remain assertive in the context.

The second version greets the eye with a compact vision. While recast in different roles, the vessels are scaled back in volume accordingly. Gone is the chic slim jug. Copious room is granted to a coffee pot as the centerpiece, bulky in burnt umber, its white patterns almost engulfed in the dark interior. The coffee pot is charming to look at, though. Its curves, lid to bottom, showcase the flowing lines at the painter's best. Its fluid depiction of the double-arched handle is breathtakingly lucid, tactful, and determined, which Matisse would have marveled at if he had ever seen them.

The trio is cut down to a

Still Life (Print 3) ca. 1940s
Lin Fengmian

Glassware ca. 1950s
Lin Fengmian

bowl-and-jug duet in the third piece (Print 3). To place the most austere version as the ending piece in this particular series reassures us about the opinion that Lin is moving toward increasing simplicity. Yet a review of his later works from 1950s through the early 1960s, a period that has seen his best works come into being, points to something different. Lin's pursuit for simplicity is not conducted in the sense that each and every painting is going to meet the standard unbendingly. For instance, his return to the beloved motifs in *Glassware* (ca. 1950s) is proof that he would never stop renovation. Fine and short white lines are moving in a trot in this great piece, leading the eye from the glassware to the floral-print draperies designed with remarkable patience. That said, the sequence of the three variations produced circa 1940s becomes no less opaque in that the notion of increasing simplicity does not befit Lin's arc of advancement that is resistant by nature to any formulaic fabrication.

Tipped up for better viewing, two mat-like pieces are spread out on the table in the third version, one put on top of the other diagonally to render the strong lines in a nice rhyme scheme. Sitting atop the surface are the fruit bowl and the patterned jug, altered this time to be blunt. Compared with the lines applied to the mat-like stuff, the lines dripping along the vessels wriggle at some points as if intent upon taking leave of form. The upper portion of the jug handle loosens in swelling ink, and the bottom of the jug is undercut audaciously. In addition, the fruit bowl is somewhat malformed as if it all happened in the phase of blowing. Intriguingly, the vaguely checked tablecloth that goes underneath is quietly textured and colored. Its checked pattern is half earthen, half grayish, elaborated in an unusual manner to encourage comparison with the austere motifs sitting atop.

Is it an attempt to create an interesting figure-ground relationship? Is it a dashed-off painting brushed up afterwards? Or is it the real initial that comes to inspire the other two versions?

It is possible to whittle down the possibilities but chances are slender to get close to the truth at this stage. False hope arose when the exhibition "Centenarian Lin Fengmian: A Pictorial Biography" (世纪风眠——林风眠画传展) was staged at National Art Museum of China in April 2016. Judging from the diluted biographical element and the mainly clichéd form of painting, its curating quality was no parallel with "Matisse in the Studio" recently held at Boston's Museum of Fine Arts, where the viewer had access to some of the objects used in his oeuvre, including the green Spanish vase restructured in *Vase of Flowers* (1924) and several other works repeatedly. To seek the vessels used by Lin during the wartime might end up all for naught because of a strong belief that Lin did not paint from life or nature during that period, but from memory, inhabited as well as imagined.